The Church
and the New Generation

The Church
and the New Generation

CHARLES E. MOWRY

ABINGDON PRESS
NASHVILLE AND NEW YORK

THE CHURCH AND THE NEW GENERATION

Copyright © 1969 by Abingdon Press

Library of Congress Catalog Card Number: 69-12013

SET UP, PRINTED, AND BOUND BY THE
PARTHENON PRESS, AT NASHVILLE,
TENNESSEE, UNITED STATES OF AMERICA

Preface

This is not a _how to_ book. It is not a quick guide to successful experiences with the new generation.

The church must change. Not because the new generation says so. Most of them aren't saying so. They don't really believe the church is capable of the kind of change that can make it a relevant institution in their lives. The church must change because obedience to its purpose demands that it change. Already many are trying. But too many—laymen, pastors, and bishops—hold back out of fear, holier-than-thou attitudes, and ignorance about the true mission of the church of Jesus Christ.

This is an attempt to call the church to further examination of its life and practice. No easy answers, no quick tricks, no supersalesmen will substitute for the necessity for the church to reexamine thoroughly its own functioning and its present-day forms. The church, according to the New Testament, is to be a dynamic, transforming force in society. It hardly measures up to that role in current American life.

But emerging cultural changes are calling for help in assessing the moral and ethical implications of the alternatives before us as a nation. The new generation sharply draws the questions and the issues. It must face the difficulties which are inevitable. It is seeking a source of support and authority for radical transformation of society. Only the church and the tradition of democracy can endorse that effort.

The church is called to cease loving itself and love the world . . . in this case the world of the new generation.

In pulling together this material, I have found inestimable assistance from my association with colleagues of the National Young Adult Project staff and those persons engaged in ministries with the new generation in cities from San Diego to Boston. I am particularly indebted to Ted McIlvenna and Lewis Durham of the Glide Urban Center in San Francisco and Dr. Allen Moore of the School of Theology, Claremont, California, who have been not only colleagues but teachers and friends. Finally, this book might never have been undertaken without the encouragement and interest which my wife, Marilyn, has given me to approach my whole efforts to understand both the church and the new generation.

Charles E. Mowry

Nashville, Tennessee
April 22, 1968

Contents

one

The Big Generation

There are nearly forty million young adults in the United States. That is more than all the people in the state of New York and the state of California combined. It is more than the total population of the United States in 1860, the time of the Civil War. The population mean is declining in spite of the increased ability to prolong human life by many years. Soon we will reach a mean age level of twenty-five; some predict twenty-four. That means that soon half the total population of the nation will be twenty-five years old or less.

During the five-year period from 1946-1950 this nation experienced something for which it was unprepared, namely, an explosion in the birth rate. Those five years produced 3,500,000 more births than the preceding five years. This generation's arrival at the nation's hospitals was big news. It has been news ever since. Even as it taxed the facilities of the hospitals and the energy level of the medical profession, it has taxed every aspect of our national life requiring and often determining priorities.

Although there are many exceptions to every generalization, the generation does take on certain predominant or significant characteristics.

BIG GENERATION—BIG PROBLEMS

Never has a generation been followed in such complete surveillance as has this generation. We have discovered that it is not only a big generation but it has created big problems from the outset. These persons have been a pressure on public facilities, an overcrowded market for particular commodities, an expanded demand on those who try to coordinate need and supply. In addition to the sudden demand for maternity facilities in the hospitals across the nation, they made demands on the suppliers of infant and child-care items. Everything from diaper pins to washing machines, from powder to playpens was suddenly in enormous demand. Whole new industries such as "diaper services" were brought into being to supply the essentials and extras of infant care.

The Educational Problems. But babies don't stay babies for long. Soon they would be knocking on the nation's school doors. How and where were all these children going to "fit" into the schools? They wouldn't! They were too numerous to handle by adding a few seats on the ends of the present rows. The population trends seemed always to exceed the curves on which the school planners were building.

The schools needed teachers; they needed elementary classrooms; they needed just about anything one can imagine except students. The old formula of one teacher and twenty-five children disappeared, if in fact it had ever been effected. The temporary classroom popped up. Then came the junior and senior high schools. Even a hurried reading of Edgar Friedenberg's *Coming of Age in America*[1] will make unquestionably clear that there is still a critical shortage of competent teachers and administrators in secondary schools.

Simultaneously education underwent a massive redirection of educational methods and procedures. There emerged an educational methodology based on the scientific process. Learning occurred most significantly when it had been acquired by asking basic questions, searching for data to shed light on questions, and formulating answers, solutions, or hypotheses.

The colleges and universities started their preparation long in advance. An emphasis on staying in school, the pressures from the job market to require college work, the emergence of whole new fields of knowledge and development all combined to present the college and university with enormous problems. Today the student population of the nation is at approximately ten million and growing. Of the total young adult population approximately 40 percent is students.

Employment Problems. The Department of Labor tries to provide the nation, especially the commercial, industrial, labor, and political sectors, with up-to-date information on the trends in the labor market. These reports have been highly evident in recent years and a matter of major concern during the 1960's.

Unemployment has a way of remaining near the 4- to 5-percent mark. That means that one of every twenty persons in the labor market is without a job. The figure has been lower at times of peak seasonal employment. The unemployment figures have enormous implications for the younger generation. Jobs are generally available to persons who are mature in preference to inexperienced or immature persons. Seniority means that layoffs affect the young first. The draft, as a demand upon the time of young men, makes them poor employment risks until they have fulfilled their obligation to the Selective Service Act. Young people have developed fewer salable skills and are ineligible for many positions.

For these reasons and more, the unemployment rate for young men and women is considerably higher than for older persons. If we use the figure of 4 percent as the national unemployment index as a reference, the unemployment of persons in the sixteen to twenty-four age range would be approximately 12 percent. Instead of one out of twenty-five, they would be unemployed at the rate of one out of eight. For young Negroes the figure takes an astounding jump to 20-25 percent, which means that between one in four or one in five young Negroes are unemployed. The Department of Labor does not include in these figures the unemployable persons.

Foundations, private business, and government have developed training programs aimed at raising the competency and skills of this unemployed population. The government offers training programs for the unemployed in a variety of packages from focusing on hard-core unemployables to area redevelopment where people in a local area are guaranteed priority for positions which have been created by new industry or business in that area.

The rolls of welfare programs include many young families and unmarried mothers with small children. Welfare may provide a child-care service which allows the mother to work and to acquire some income. Medical care is often available through welfare services. But becoming a welfare recipient reinforces a personal failure image at a time when young citizens need to be finding their *worth*.

Some would contend that Vietnam has been used to solve this domestic problem by drawing more and more young men into military service, thus improving the unemployment rolls. Sooner or later, we will stop warring, and then we can anticipate that three efforts will be made simultaneously: (1) We will see Congress approve an enlarged standing army; (2) we will see enormous subsidies made available to induce young veterans to enter colleges and universities; and (3) we will see renewed emphasis placed on programs such as the Peace Corps and VISTA.

Finally, many contend that viewing the economic situation through employment-unemployment glasses is obsolete. They believe all men and women must have personal purchasing power to maintain an active economy. They have recommended to the President of the United States that a program of *guaranteed annual income* be established to assure every citizen a minimum annual wage whether employed or not.[2]

Other solutions to the unemployment problem suggest more conventional means. In order to combat the unemployment of the Negro population, the Equal Opportunities Employment Program is now in effect. Churches have begun attempts to support this program through the Roman Catholic plan known as Project Equality. An ugly picture has been uncovered in many places because churches have been so dependent on racist-dominated members and contributors that they have been afraid to join forces in Project Equality. The new generation sees and knows what this says about the church.

Wherever unemployment is a factor, it is a young adult crisis.

A Place to Live. Housing has been big business in the United States for the last twenty years. In the city of Dallas it is estimated that there is a continuing need of eight thousand apartment units each year to keep up with demand. Entire sections of older residential areas have gone under the ball of the wrecker and the blade of the dozer as land is cleared for new luxurious garden apartments. Many apartments cater exclusively to the young adult population. They sometimes provide a separate complex for single young adults and another for young marrieds. The apartments offer swimming pools, recreation areas, private clubs or bars (depending on alcohol laws), game rooms, party rooms, outdoor charcoal cookers, laundries, bowling teams or leagues, and periodic house parties, sponsored by the management, for all occupants.

Dormitories are another kind of housing in which many young adults live. Colleges and universities represent a mixed pattern of attitudes toward dormitories today. Some schools still attempt to provide housing. At the other extreme are those schools who have, by policy, gone out of (or never entered) the housing business. Some of these schools are the newer universities, colleges, junior colleges, and community colleges. Many of them anticipate student bodies of ten and twenty thousand but do not plan to provide student housing.

While there are some very good reasons, economic and otherwise, for the university to cease being a dorm mother or father, large numbers of students are often victims of circumstance as they find or fail to find adequate housing at a fair price. Volunteer organizations or local service organizations must help stabilize costs and establish certain criteria for satisfactory accommodations. Many students arrive at college with little skill in handling their own affairs. Some need simple referral and assistance in getting located and situated.

RIGHTS! RIGHTS! RIGHTS!

No problem that has emerged with the present generation is more controversial or more explosive than the question of rights. Whether it is due to the coincidence of the civil rights movement or whether it is that the members of this generation have learned to live a life with considerably more freedom than their parents, one thing is sure—they believe that they have some freedoms and that those freedoms assure them of certain rights. They believe that all people are assured certain rights, and many are as displeased when someone else seems to be losing his rights as they are when they feel that their own rights and freedoms are being restricted or denied.

The issue of rights seems to have surfaced in four categories—civil, legal, right of dissent, and privacy.

The Civil Rights Movement. This was most visible in the early sixties. The manpower of the young black and the young white was as essential to the successes of the movement as was its older leadership. The civil rights cause won the support of much of the young generation without reservation. Here was a struggle against a concept which they were convinced was obsolete for a democracy. The Negro was to gain his equal status, his basic freedom from procedures like "separate but equal"; he was to assume a place in the intercurrents of national life whether in politics, economics, education, transportation, services, or employment. It was a cause—something which deserved an all-out effort, risk-taking, and sacrifice. The generation showed a fearful and skeptical public that basic rights and freedoms could be assured to a whole sector of national life from whom such rights had been denied for two hundred years.

They sang "We Shall Overcome," and they did! They hoped to form a more perfect democracy and to grant life more fully to the American Negro. They tasted victory. They will not soon forget that, when someone tries, freedom can be acquired for those who have not yet received it.

Another civil rights area is the homophile community. It is the total homosexual population including lesbians (females). Estimates of the number of these persons in the United States vary widely. One report predicts that the total homophile population in the United States by 1970 will be eighteen million. Other figures tend to be more conservative. An accurate figure is impossible, but this is a very significant minority. The largest number are young adults.

I raise this matter of rights in this context because the

greater part of the homosexual world is composed of young men and women. Many of them carry their names on church rolls. Almost all of them, though there are exceptions, feel we do not want them in our church activities; yet the great majority are respectable, disciplined, moral persons with responsible jobs and clear-thinking judgment. They feel that both the church and the larger society prefer to deny that they are there or believe that, if they wanted to, they could change their way of life. These attitudes held by the church and the society are being brought to question by the new generation.[3]

Legal Rights. Two illustrations. First, there are today in every big city numerous trade, technical, and business schools. In almost every city one can discover schools whose practices bear a second look. For example, a school will enroll students, require advance registration fees, and announce class schedules. Students pay their fees and arrange a part-time job in the hours not scheduled for classes. Then suddenly the class is rescheduled by the school to an hour inconvenient to many students. To continue that particular class would require dropping their part-time job. They can't afford that, so they must drop the course and forfeit the fee. Then they may have to attend an extra term to complete their work, thus paying an additional fee. Or they adjust, attend the course, and find that the teacher is irregular—in some cases even incompetent to provide them an adequate understanding of the skill or information they must learn from the course.

These schools often offer a lifetime employment service. Students and former students may rely on the school to refer them to a potential employer for interview. In practice some schools have an infamous record of slow response. Applicants sometimes wait weeks without assistance. When they seek employment in some other route, they are told that the school was on a good lead for them but they acted too hurriedly and should have waited for the school employment service.

The time has come for moral leadership in every city to evaluate the practices of trade, technical, and business schools. Where there are questions, thorough probing should be done. If necessary, state assemblies should make provisions which guarantee the student his or her legal rights.

Second is the legal question of voting age. This issue seems to be raised most sharply in times of war because the older generation is then more guilt conscious (not that the guilt doesn't exist at other times) of the use they are making of the young. When old men use young men for targets (and soldiers) to settle the problems they have been unable or unwilling to settle otherwise, one can be sure that at least some of those old men will begin to wonder if the least they might do is also include the young in exercising a voice in public policies at home. But the old men will never do more than talk about it. Action will come only when the young organize to demand and fight for it. They want a voice in a society that almost takes control of them from age six. That control is exercised by *required* participation in various kinds of institutions—primarily the schools, bolstered by courts, jails, and military service.

The voting question is going to take on the shape of a cause one day, and when it does there will be a violent conflict, as most of the old men will fear granting the young power and a voice in the affairs of the national life. In January of 1967, President Johnson, speaking to a group of young citizens gathered in Washington, made his famous "butt-in" invitation. He advised them that he needed them, that their voice was essential to national policy; and then, instead of guaranteeing them a voice in either the American government or his own party politics, he left them with the idea that if they get in they'll have to "butt" their way in. Some of Mr. Johnson's colleagues of younger years will live to see it happen, whether they like it or not. The young are students of power today. They understand it; they are getting experience in organizing to utilize it; and one day soon they will hold sufficient power to incite further action.

The Right of Dissent. We have seen our senators, our congressmen, the cabinet secretaries, and other national figures move to express their opinions on the right of dissent. They have come out in favor, in opposition, and in-between. The time has come when this is sufficiently a national issue that national figures can no longer avoid taking some stand regarding it. The extremes might be illustrated by Lewis B. Hershey, of the Selective Service Commission, and the late Senator Robert F. Kennedy. Mr. Hershey, a retired general, advocates that all dissenters of the Vietnam war should be immediately drafted into the Army and sent there to fight. One wonders what he thinks an army is for! Since when did an army become society's arm for discipline and retaliation against a citizen with a minority opinion? Under the right conditions Mr. Hershey might require military service for all the hippies, the black power advocates, the rioters, the homosexuals, long-haired intellectuals, and go-go girls . . . what an army! Senator

19

Kennedy, on the other hand, clearly chose to take the position of a dissenter, himself, in regard to national policies when he entered the presidential contest in 1968.

Another area of dissent emerges on the university campus in regard to the authority and power a university exercises over students. Is a university empowered to act as parent, as legal guardian, and as enforcer of moral preferences, traditional practices of one group or another, and so forth? It was this group of questions, along with others, that was being raised by the Free Speech Movement at Berkeley, California, a few years ago. More recently these questions have been sharply raised across the continent at Columbia. And these same questions are in themselves *dissent*. But is dissent permissible? Is it a right of a citizen? Under what circumstances and how much power can be exercised in the effort to dissent against another opinion? What obligation is there in our society for the two parties or sides of a controversial issue to negotiate their problem jointly?

We are living in a time of transition from one set of institutions to a set of revamped or entirely new institutions. The exercise of the dissenting voice will be increasingly with us. We will be assisted by it if we can arrive at some understanding about the rights and privileges and responsibilities of dissenters.

The Matter of Privacy. We must find a way to guarantee both generations some privacy. We cannot constantly be looking down our noses at our sons and daughters advising them to "cut their hair," "wear longer skirts," "do this," "stop that." Does the student who pays his dormitory rent have authority over what happens in his room? Or does the university set the rules of conduct for the privacy of one's own living quarters?

The right of privacy stems directly from the Bill of Rights. Those first ten amendments to the Constitution of the United States were placed there to protect the individual from the power of the government. It seems that, if the procedure of our land is that the government cannot make laws which invade the privacy of people, then lesser institutions should not attempt to exercise such controls either.

Privacy is important to most people if for no other reason than the right to "get away from it all" for a time to get things into some kind of larger perspective. It assures individuals and groups that they can withdraw from the activity of the day-to-day life and carefully determine the meaning of contemporary events. They can draw their own conclusions. They are not required to accept any other person's or group's interpretation. The United States Supreme Court declared in the case of Board of Education vs. Barnette, 319 US 624 that "if there is any fixed star in our constitutional constellation, it is that no official, high or petty, can prescribe what shall be orthodox in politics, nationalism, religion, or other matters of opinion or force citizens to confess by word or act their faith therein." William O. Douglas, a Justice of the Supreme Court, comments that "unfortunately, however, in recent years we seem to have lost sight of this 'fixed star.' The past twenty years have seen an increasing tendency to inquire into beliefs and opinions, and to impose penalties on those who hold beliefs which do not conform to the views of the majority." [4]

21

The real danger which is present in a society that guarantees individual privacy is that the individuals will choose privacy over social responsibility. When that occurs, the stagnation of a society has begun. People with differing views cease to confront one another in open discussion of critical issues. They withdraw, become indifferent, and the social order is fragmented. The common good is no longer the goal. I fear this has been happening in America.

There is no law which requires that persons must enter into dialogue with one another. And this absence of dialogue is a danger today. Some of the motivation toward privacy is a desire to live within a privatistic world without regard for others or the future. This attitude can only lead to the kind of estrangement and distance which requires open conflict for the persons on one side of the chasm to get the attention of those on the other side. Negotiations cannot be undertaken until the individual is somehow drawn out of his "shell." So, as we live with a generation gap, the adult society directed toward privatism and withdrawal from any potential conflict, we are headed for some kind of demonstration by the young to get the attention of the older generation. For the hippies it is dress and values. For the young black power advocate it is fire and riot. For the more conventional young person it is commitment to the dreams of men like King, McCarthy, and Kennedy. It is essential that communication occur, as we live in a time when old institutions are being tested and judged as useless and new institutions are being established. Privacy, rightly exercised, can contribute to the creativity of this process.

A GENERATION OF DOERS

The culture has a way of labeling each generation of young people as they begin to move into the adult world. There was the "uncommitted" generation, then the "conformist" generation, then the "beat" generation, and now a generation of "doers." Today's generation is in many ways exactly what so many public voices lamented an absence of in the past several generations. It used to be said, we need young people with drive, who dream great dreams and believe in them and are willing to do something about them. The beats, the dropouts, the conformers, the uncommitted, and all their likes were big disappointments. We wondered what would happen to our world, our democracy, our freedoms, our history, and the future of our nation and land. We wanted a generation of young people who cared. We wanted them to care while they were young.

Well! What do you think!

Today we have a generation with many faces. There are a sizable number of conformists. Probably the largest single group are those who are trying to find their place, get through college or high school, be nice, keep a clean record, take a job, marry, have babies, buy automobiles, and get a Playboy key. And we've got dropouts—they're dropping out of anything that is controversial. They're dropping into the stream of mundane life that some of the adult world has so ably provided. They stand for nothing; they do as little as possible; they don't respond to the great human cries of our age, whether it's the United Fund or the Negro ghetto child or the peace movement or the UN. They just lie there (sit, walk, talk when you pull the string). They go to work and don't rock the boat. They go to the club and don't rock the boat. If they go to church, they don't rock the boat there either.

The people of this generation who are setting a pace for our culture are the "doers." It's been a long, long time since America had a generation of doers. It has seldom had doers like these. These doers may represent a minority attitude, as doers always do, but they're going to make a difference which is immeasurable. They may be few in thousands, but they are everywhere. They are scattered throughout the Latin and African and Asian worlds with the faces and hearts and hands of the Peace Corpsmen. They are scattered in the deprived areas of our own land as the VISTA workers. They are collected in the great cities of our land, living a strange kind of life, labeled "hippies." They are ridiculed, but deep down inside those real hippies (to be differentiated from the kids who just grow long hair and practice exhibitionism) are working on the meaning of life in a world where people are educated and can't plan to spend most of their day on a job somewhere. They are the dark confident faces of the black power movement and the efforts at community organization of the poor. They are the lighter, confident faces of the Students for a Democratic Society in the ghettos of all colors. They are the multi-colored faces of the new political left. They are the trip cult. They are the bright, insightful people who staff the National Student Association and a hundred other organizations and movements from coast to coast.

They are different beyond their activism. Every generation has had its minority of activists. But generally those activists found and accepted invitations to go to work inside one of the mighty institutions of their time, be it YMCA or

24

church or social work agencies. This generation's activists have deliberately chosen to decline "buying in" with us who are older. They're different. They believe that, if they are going to make a mark on our society, they have to do it from a different set of perceptions and assumptions. And they look at people of my generation and discover, or are reminded, that buying in is a very, very slow and perhaps impossible change process. Too slow for the rate of change which is happening in other aspects of our culture and society.

So they are struggling for better routes to "the action"—action that must take place. They have some advantages available to them that weren't available to earlier generations. They can stay in communication with one another. They can fly to any city in a few hours. They can maintain a communication system which gives them firsthand information on any issue anywhere. They can be at the grass roots of our society. They can live with the poor, the Negro, the mountaineer, the outcast. They can stand before the Capitol or the Oakland Terminal or the sheriff of Selma or the President of Columbia, or the Secretary of State. They can be present when and where the action occurs. They can inject themselves into the tides of history as they emerge. They can, by doing so, participate in forming history in ways that have never been available before to anyone, regardless of age or station. And they are doing it!

These young people are educated. They comprehend the mass media in ways far more perceptive than those of us who are older. They are more inclined to act out their opinions. They live for the now, realizing that tomorrow can only begin with what it inherits from today. They utilize devices of the communications field as if they have been here always. For example, SNCC is reported to have a teletype system to every major city where it has staff at work. In San Francisco a group of the "doers" founded The Communications Company, which operated around the clock to get out word to everyone in the Haight-Ashbury area on any topic which seemed important. The messages were direct, simple, and dealt with an issue of crucial importance. Copying machines, computers, television cameras, major magazine publishers have all fallen victim to the desire and skill of the various movements of this generation and have told their story for them in ways and to publics that they could have never reached within the resources of their own system. They comprehend the complexity and operations of the contemporary world better than most of us who are past thirty. Through flexible and imaginative use of the resources which they have to draw upon, they have been able to establish and maintain communication between local people, national networks, and where needed, international communications.

A GENERATIONAL IDENTITY

Many observers have speculated that this generation seems to have a kind of unity or distinctive identity. Some describe it as a generational subculture. In any event, there seem to be a number of threads which generally run throughout the generation.

A Common Inheritance. The forceful element of the generation is made up predominantly of people with middle-class values and resources. They have been bombarded since childhood with television and radio and film communication which has portrayed life as it exists for the great middle class, so that even those who come from lower-class environments often understand the middle-class ways, at least as well as they understand their own. And those from the upper class seem often to be trying to find their way into the acceptance of the middle group. This has resulted in providing them with a common perspective on history and events. They have acquired perspective via the interpreters of the three big networks and the major news services. They have acquired their attitudes by the kind of conditioning that comes from the mass communication media. They have been formed by these impersonal but "reliable" systems and services.

With this common history or inheritance—its world view —the generation has a kind of unity on which contemporary life is viewed and weighed. A part of that common history has been the radical rate of change which has occurred. It has often left young adults to face new problems without any assistance from parents, teachers, clergymen, or other adults. They have discovered that permissiveness, freedom to doubt and question and weigh alternative responses, is a more desirable environment in which to shape a life which must constantly adapt to new realities. More desirable, that is, than the environment of the older world, where principles are somehow often more absolute than is the reality of change which is occurring. The older generation's determination to have some absolute values makes adjusting to current change a difficulty, if not an impossibility.

The result has been a widespread interdependence

27

among peers who are experiencing the initial impact of these transitional demands in their own lives. This common searching and interdependence further strengthen the unity or common identity which seems to be emerging.

In Search of a Place. It has probably never been easy for a rising generation to find and take its place in the world which exists about it. Time may prove that it has been easier for this contemporary rising generation than for some of those who preceded it. It may be that it is easier to get "in" in a society in intense transition than in a stable society with little change being effected. But, whether that be true or not, persons in this new generation do feel the need to find a place for themselves, both as individuals and as a generation. It is not possible to describe the "place" for which they are looking, for it is many places. Some are seeking security, some adventure, some danger, some revolution, some reform, some quiet, some the multimedia impact, some the expanded mind, some the status of prominence, some a mystical faith, some power, some wisdom, and so on.

But the search for some place is a common bond. In the stable society places seemed to be numbered, and, if one place was vacated, then someone would step in and fill it again. Today we have whole fields of professional expertise in which all the people are the first generation in that field. The top positions as well as the bottom ones are filled by people only a few years out of university. Whole new fields of engineering, science, and technology have been born in the past ten years. There are no vacancies due to someone older dropping out. The whole thing is one grand vacancy.

Likewise, whole professions or occupational fields may suddenly vanish from the scene as have the elevator operator, the street sweeper with a push broom, the blacksmith.

In times like this, seeking a place requires much more self-direction. It is not unusual for the situation to change drastically, even as one is attempting a solution of a given situation. For example, several years ago Dallas voted to install an alert system. While its leaders were making studies, taking bids, and installing the system, intercontinental missiles were perfected, so that before it was fully installed it was obsolete, thus requiring the whole attempt to start again from scratch. This does require that decisions be made promptly. The decisions should be made in light of a variety of data which must be pulled together for immediate action. In our time the demand for prompt decisions should not necessarily imply that those decisions might have a larger margin of error. Rather, it may be that with new means of information, retrieval, and storage, decisions can be more quickly made and also made better.

Finding a place requires knowledge of the "scene" and the ability to make one's decisions and act upon them immediately. If one waits alongside the action today, he may discover that there are no places left. There can be no doubt but that with the transitional times there has been an increase of competitiveness for the "places" in which persons can find meaning and satisfaction in their daily work and effort.

Looking for a "place" also relates to something bigger. It is the search for oneself in the string of events which makes history. It is the desire for a place where the generation as a whole can affect that history. Will the generation finally measure up as a "doer" generation? Or will it eventually prove to be a pretender generation? Or an active generation with inaccurate or unuseful goals?

It appears to me that this generation is going to hold a pivotal place in national history. If it is handled well and effectively, it may prove to be much more, perhaps a pivotal place in human history itself. For history is taking some radical departures because of the technological and automated progress of the last two decades. Where it is taking us we can only speculate, but one thing is sure—it will be in the hands and minds of this rising generation.

A GENERATION GAP

As all this occurs, there will be a widening of what is already identified as a *gap* between the generations. The gap, in its basic form, is one related to values and morality. The older generation has a set of values which have been institutionalized effectively into the various structures of the day from the federal government to churches to economic structures. The new generation seems to have serious doubt about these values and their related institutions. Young adults are reluctant to give support to the institutions, and thus the values.

The striking content of the gap is one of values. The new generation is coming forth with a set of values which can only be described as "of no kinship" to the set of values held most widely by its fathers. Whether one wants to explore religious practice, political ideology, governmental authority, individual freedom, international affairs, legal reform, business ethics, education, or whatever, he is most likely to get a new set of assumptions to which will be added a new set of perceptions, with the outcome calling not for a revision of the older value but a discarding of it and a new, often radical, replacement.

two

Profile of the Young Adult

There is no doubt that this current new generation has been studied more thoroughly than any preceding generation. We know a great deal about their school life, their economic purchasing power, their likes and dislikes in consumer items, their population and distribution, and special statistics on those who marry, divorce, commit crimes, belong to militant organizations. But, when we come to the intangibles of their beliefs and values and attitudes, we can only conclude that up to the present time researchers and behavioral scientists have shied away from such studies. No doubt numerous single-factor studies have been conducted by graduate students in universities, but such studies often have limited value and are generally not available.[1] We have very few data to help us assess the meaning of the post–high school experience on the values, beliefs, and attitudes of American youth.

However, the younger generation has always been a concern of the older generations, regardless of what seems to be occurring in human history. Such a concern is today greatly focused in the context of the urbanization, computerization, and mass nature of current life. In a real sense the older generations have always considered their offspring as something of a problem, a danger, as somehow being unqualified to gain their inevitable inheritance. One can find records of such concern in literature that is 2,500 years old. The Old Testament's book of Proverbs reads:

My son, hear the instruction of thy father,
And forsake not the law of thy mother:
For they shall be an ornament of grace unto thy head,
   and chains about thy neck.
My son, if sinners entice thee, consent thou not.
If they say, Come with us,
   let us lay in wait for blood.
let us lurk privily for the innocent without cause:
   Let us swallow them up alive as the grave; and whole,
   as those that go down into the pit:
We shall find all precious substance, we shall fill our houses
   with spoil:
Cast in thy lot among us; let us all have one purse:
My son, walk not thou in the way with them; refrain thy foot
   from their path:
For their feet run to evil, and make haste to shed blood.
                        (Prov. 1:8-16.)

Even though hard data are not available to provide an accurate picture of the generation, attempts must be made to grasp the core of young adults' life styles and the patterns ot living and attitudes held by them. Some broad, generalized characteristics are offered here, again acknowledging that in every instance it will be easy for the reader to lift data of an exactly opposing characteristic.

UNIFORMITY VS. DIVERSITY

There is no overall uniformity in the new generation. It can be viewed from a thousand and one different angles or perspectives, and each one may be somewhat accurate and at the same time inaccurate if one attempts to make it apply to all. What can be identified are some major streams of attitudes, values, beliefs, and behaviors.

PEERS VS. ELDERS

Young adults are drawn to peers. Careful observers often agree that persons in this generation are more universally drawn to their peers than preceding ones. Reason for this is laid to the unique history and life experience these have had, in which they have always lived in a world of perceptions which never have been and never will be like those of their fathers. This is especially true of young Americans. They have been formed by influences which were not a part of the formation of their parents. They have learned differently and generally with little help from Mom or Dad. They have discovered through the mass communication media that they are citizens of the world, not just citizens of a nation. They also avail themselves of the resources of the technological and "ditto-ized" processes, so that Sgt. Pepper's Band is "their music" whether they are hippies in the East Village or college students at

Vanderbilt or young sailors in San Diego or weekend customers of the In Crowd in Dallas.

A series of interviews with young adults today will reveal that in the great majority of instances the young feel they have very little in common with their parents in areas of political policy, national policy, and questions of freedom and rights. Most express reservations indicating that they have learned to avoid these topics when visiting with parents. They have almost no common ground on which to discuss the crises of our national and personal life today.

This dependence on the acceptance and support of the peer group begins long before young adulthood. It plays a major part in life formation which goes on during adolescence. With the peer group having become an established and meaningful, as well as worthwhile, reference, it should not be underrated in understanding these same persons as they move into an adult society which isn't ready for them, their ideas, and their perceptions. J. E. Horrocks writes of the earlier influence of peer groups:

Research has suggested that within the group situation the adolescent can feel a sense of power, belonging and security; . . . The rewards of prestige and freedom of movement seem to be more valid if bestowed by the group and it is, perhaps, because of this that group influence can overwhelm and negate parental instructions and prohibitions.

Thus, we may see the peer world, for most adolescents, as a tremendously important source of attitudes, the inhibitor as well as the initiator of action, the arbitrator of right and wrong, and the dispenser of acceptance and rejection. . . . The peer group has the further function of acting as a proving ground—a place to test oneself, to try things out, and to learn to cope with others.

Tryon writes of the peer group, "It is in this by *doing* they learn about the social processes of our culture. They clarify their sex roles by acting and being responded to, they learn competition, cooperation, social skills, values and purposes by sharing the common life." [2]

Of course, our culture is designed to provide a young man or woman maximum time with and availability to peers. The high schools, social clubs, suburbs of similarly aged families, colleges, military, prisons, apartments, and even many working situations make peers available in great quantities, and the confining nature of life in these situations makes peer relationships quite intense. It would be interesting to see what might occur if our culture were oriented to intergenerational groupings rather than peer groupings. But for the present not only is the peer grouping deemed desirable so far as the young person is concerned, but the adult society which determines and supports the societal structures sees it to be advantageous to the whole in spite of the numerous remarks to the contrary by many of the leaders themselves. They go right on reinforcing groupings and social structures designed to converge people as peers.

Peer groupings feed a shifting of interests, opinions, attitudes, and finally values. This rightfully becomes a great concern of the adult generation. Adults are intuitively aware that, whenever the values which they hold and expect to remain the primary values of the society are met with indifference and disregard, we are in for a value revolution. And that revolution will have a radical effect on the basic functioning of society, its institutions and established operating systems. Values cannot change without institutions

36

changing also, for institutions are created to maintain a particular value or system of values.

ANTI-ESTABLISHMENT POSTURE

Much of the adult-controlled and -directed society has been labeled the Establishment. Young adults are themselves anti-Establishment. I quote Dr. Rosemary Parks, President of Barnard College.

I do not mean by this that the younger generation is in rebellion against us. I do not mean that they reject us. There is a third possibility, and that is the stance in which I think they find themselves today. They consider us irrelevant. . . . They have cast us in the role of something they call the "Establishment." The Establishment for them is the embodiment of every form of compromise in politics, economics, and social and personal life.[3]

This anti-Establishment posture is not something which can be laughed off. It is not going away because many adults have chosen to disregard it. It is widespread, and it seems to be almost all inclusive of the power efforts made by the adult society toward the younger generation.

Let me try to illustrate the presence of the Establishment as its opponents view it. They wonder when the truth might come forth to bridge the credibility gap in the executive branch of national government. Only at the time of this writing has someone finally come forth to make a public statement that the counsel received by President John F. Kennedy regarding the Bay of Pigs "invasion" was poor counsel, that they all goofed in that decision. What the younger generation suspected was, in fact, true! They would like to have equally honest answers about Guatemala, about the economic crisis over gold, about Vietnam, about the Selective Service Act, about the spy ship *Pueblo*, taken by North Korea, about the desire for peace in the world, about the policies of referring problems to the United Nations, about revision of laws regarding marijuana, about the assassination of John Kennedy, about the influence of wealthy men over city and state political issues, and on and on.

The issue of credibility has become more than a gap. With the new generation it is a gulf, and bridging it daily is becoming less likely. I recall the Smothers Brothers, themselves spokesmen of the new generation, in their Comedy Hour show in early 1968. When discussing possible uses of the old London Bridge, which was to be sold to the highest bidder, one brother suggested that the United States government might buy it to help bridge the credibility gap! In both electricity and mountain climbing, a gap is a place where crossing is possible. I do not see very many of the articulate, vocal leaders of the new generation with much hope that this gap can be crossed. They are proceeding as if credibility must be recovered, reestablished—*by them.* The Establishment's policies of news control and ill-informed executive decisions under the guise of national welfare or international interests have left us a nation of people who are increasingly unable to exercise an informed vote, even though we have a process of democratic elections. Or so the younger generation is saying. This crisis which the younger generation experiences today, according to William Stringfellow, is clearly not specifically their own moral decadence of absence of purpose or bewilderment. The crisis of youth and, for that matter, the crisis of their elders, today concerns the unreliability, corruption, and obsolescence of many of the inherited institutions, policies, laws, standards, and presuppositions of this society.

The sins of the fathers may be visited upon the sons, but that does not thereby absolve the fathers.⁴

Nor does it solve the broken conditions of the son's inheritance. He, too, must struggle to create some order and meaning out of the pieces which he knows about and the missing pieces which have been withheld from him.

The Establishment is the college or university that neglects basic education of students in its expectations for faculty to publish or to earn grants for research and study. It is the high school that is more skilled in the arts of discipline and management of large numbers of adolescents than it is in teaching contemporary history and its moral and ethical issues. It is the unchecked causes that make young Negroes unable to find work and driven to stealing in order to feed a young wife or buy shoes for a new baby. It is the system that makes records for people in police stations who were arrested mistakenly, but two years later reports that the individual "has a record with the police." It is the authorities and the system that make it necessary for a Negro mother to ask her husband to leave the house and no longer live there in order for them to acquire a few more dollars on which to live. It is the system which advocates that young men who oppose our policies in Vietnam be immediately reclassified for induction. It is the system that provides no alternative to a young woman who has become pregnant except to have an unwanted child and add one more digit to a population explosion already feared as an eminent crisis in our world today. It is the system that keeps young Negro families from living where they can afford homes because whites are afraid. It is the system that sends poor teachers to the very underprivileged students who get no help at home in trying to acquire an education. It is a system that uses churches as a front for its own corrupted and privatistic values. The church, as we will see in the next chapter, is viewed as a major partner in the Establishment enterprise.

CRISIS IN GOALS AND LOYALTIES

It is likely that the larger section of the new generation population is best described as *apathetic,* evidencing *anomie* and a general *infidelity.* The apathy is probably a result of living in a time when the answers to the problems that a person experiences aren't available without personal searching and struggle. Most of these young men and women are not accustomed to exerting a tremendous effort in order to accomplish whatever it is they happen to face. Studies indicate that this attitude is held by most of the students in colleges, as well as those who have not attended college and many who have not finished high school. It becomes apparent that they are not particularly conditioned to a strong will to solve problems, set high goals, and pursue them.

There are those in the church who would have us believe that the young adults who are actively related to local churches should be viewed as the troops of a beachhead force of young churchmen which can somehow "win the new generation to the church's side." That is utterly unrealistic. The very nature of these people implies that they are *not* strong, able leaders in groups where conflict and feelings are dealt with openly.

Studies of persons in young adult church groups indicate that these persons are more likely to be dependent, dogmatic, and generally insecure and indecisive. They are in these groups because they do not have the personal confidence and initiative to be out with the rest of their own generation. Few are able to understand themselves enough to recognize this, but serious study of the groups and the persons will establish the situation to any careful observer. The beachhead theory proposes that churches which have young adults today use them to contact and hold ties with the rest of the younger generation. The simple situation is that the rest of the generation is not going to follow these persons anywhere, much less to a church likely to be clearly a part of the Establishment. These young adults are what Roy Larson calls "young fogies."

I wish the beachhead theory were a live option. Many churches are still trying to make it work. But success is a rare exception indeed. Still many people, from local laity to national connectional secretaries, persist in advocating this procedure. It is ill-informed advice by people who seek easy answers to difficult questions. Either they are so separated from the problem that they do not know that many churches are trying this already with disappointing results, or they feel that those attempting it aren't competent to give the theory a real try. I know many competent people who are failing with this effort. It isn't the question of competency, it is a poor theory for today's church. Those who continue to advocate it as a solution do the church and the new generation a real disservice.

Infidelity can be seen in the transitional nature of loyalties. As Malcomb Knowles reminded a national consultation recently, "Our times are marked with a *temporariness* about most everything we do or believe." [5] It is this characteristic which Edgar Friedenberg referred to in writing, "The essence of our era is a kind of infidelity, a disciplined expediency." [6]

This all relates to the posture of relative values and loyalties. However, we must not assume this automatically implies a widespread weakness in the generation. It seems to be a sign of some awareness of the mode of relativity in which we live today, as well as a kind of indecisiveness about the ability of the younger generation to give loyalty to anyone or anything over a prolonged period. It may in fact represent an absence of any clearly perceived long-range goals or objectives of the persons or the society. The absence of loyalties and the apathy are very closely related. On this particular characteristic Dr. Paul Abels writes,

The majority of contemporary American youth . . . are complacent, self-centered and apathetic about current issues and events. . . . The term "privatism" [has been coined] to represent this pattern of attitudes and values. . . . Privatism is defined as the inclination to seek a rich, full life for oneself within one's immediate family and community, to think in concrete and practical terms about material benefits that one expects to attain and enjoy, and to exhibit a pronounced unconcern with social problems and the wider world. Sixty to eighty percent of the college population endorse the key features of privatism. [7]

Integrity has a close relationship to fidelity. Both stand out in the studies of the American prisoners held by the North Korean government in the mid-1950's. The prisoners were studied extensively, and it was discovered that they were apathetic, too. Not one ever escaped. They were indifferent to one another, even to the point of taking a sick man's food from him rather than helping him eat. They could not be motivated by a sense of being soldiers or being Americans. They let health standards decline to serious levels with no desire even to maintain personal health habits which were available to them such as washing their clothing or bathing.

In all likelihood they were no different from any other group of young Americans who might have been put under the same conditions.

We may not think much of the manhood of the recent Korean captives. Judged by the standards we like to believe we hold, they fail. But it is we who have allowed those standards to become obsolete. In our social institutions, the kind of character structure that is actually nurtured to full development is very different from the kind we profess to esteem most highly. In the process of growing up many of our youth lose their integrity —or fail to develop it—because they actually have very little opportunity to learn that integrity is valuable, and a great deal of opportunity to learn that it is a luxury they probably cannot afford.

Can they afford it? Is it worth having in the modern world? In an extreme situation, the death rate among Korean prisoners suggests we cannot live without it. But men do not develop the qualities an extreme situation demands unless those qualities are of some value in their daily lives. Human growth occurs gradually. If integrity is not encouraged from day to day, one can hardly expect men to display it in emergencies.[8]

CHANGE VS. STATUS QUO

Young adults view *change as a normative element* of their environment and their own response to that changing world. Change comes in the form of social transition. It also comes through the world of values and loyalties. "The youth of today have grown up in a world of relative and changing values. The influence of such men as Freud in the field of psychiatry and Einstein in physics has had a profound effect upon social, religious, political and economic theory." [9] As the social aspects of the society undergo change, the institutions which have been established to incorporate and maintain the former way or situation must also undergo change. For example, the laws in the recent civil rights issues have instituted social change regarding both the rights and also the place of the American Negro in our society. One cannot require that major organizations become Equal Opportunity Employers without changing radically those institutions which once were not operating on such employment policies and procedure. Equal opportunity means that some Negroes will soon sit in on policy decisions, and, as they are present, new perspectives will be added and taken into account in decisions. As Negroes assume positions providing advanced income, they will want to insure better neighborhoods and schools for their children, and the integration of neighborhoods and subdivisions will become a much greater center of change. It cannot be helped. We cannot make social change in employment and economic affairs unless the other institutions of the city will soon reexamine their basic assumptions and make changes in keeping with the newer formation of the place of Negroes in society.

44

The new generation sees the change in the social and institutional arenas as "the way things are." They have not lived in a time which was characterized by static or stable social conditions. They expect things to change, and have, in many instances, assumed that their role in this age is to participate in the efforts that bring changes to fruition. They often find themselves caught by the desires of their elders for some end to the change. They find most adults unable to cope with continuing change.

Some young adults are fully in sympathy with the older generation and hope only for an end to this era of change. They are seeking absolutes. As a result, they are often led to believe that the answers to today's problems lie in some simplified answer rooted in the past, in religious postures, or in extremely narrow and unbending world views such as those offered by the John Birch Society and others.

It is likely that the new generation people differ sharply from their elders in regard to their expectations about change. Young adults seem more able to live with temporariness. They can maintain a temporariness about their ties to families, to colleges, certainly to military service, and more temporariness seems to be manifesting itself in their interpersonal relationships. More young couples choose to live together regularly without marrying, since they feel that they are in a relationship which is temporary and they do not want to get involved in all the legal entanglements necessary to terminate a marriage. Others who do marry seem to also feel that, if a marriage relationship has run into trouble, the ties are temporary—for so long as they are meaningful—and that, when meaning ceases to be a part of the relationship, the marriage should promptly be terminated.

People in the new generation generally have more friends than their parents, but these friendships are on a level which has less depth. Their relationship to parents and other adults is seen as one which must be maintained in a very controlled manner. The relationship to parents is not allowed to have the strength to overpower one with attitudes which are not acceptable to the younger generation.

Yet the happy fact remains that the emergence of a personally committed generation seeking basic social change is momentous. They are a minority of their own age group, to be sure, but a creative, activist minority who should place their stamp upon the times. Eventually, and it will probably try the anarchist spirit of some of them, they are going to lead adult movements and change this society.[10]

The late sixties bore out that Congressman John V. Tunney of southern California was correct in his prediction that the readiness for change of some of the young will try their anarchist spirit. The riots of the great ghettos of our American cities have been almost wholly manned by members of this new generation. They, wanting to change the society, have had so few avenues for facing their own problems that they have been driven to desperate ends in an attempt to get a hearing and to achieve serious recognition of their determination that change must be instituted in the ghettos.

Young adults believe they have a right to be heard, and they intend to be heard. The question for the adult society is, are we big enough to sit down and hear what they have to say, even though they haven't lived as long as we have? Are we ready to hear from them, the way life is there, in their world, and what they expect to be done about it? Strange as it may seem, they have somehow grown up to believe that American citizens should have a voice in the priorities of the government. They have grown up believing that leaders should represent the concerns of all the people and that, in order to do so, leaders must know the problems of all people. They do not believe that leaders know *their* problems or understand their perceptions of contemporary problems. They have not been able to get leaders to sit down with them and discuss their problems. They have not had places on committees and commissions to work toward resolution of problems which they see as having a direct bearing on the nature of life they will be enabled to live tomorrow. They are determined. They know that power speaks. Money is power, but they have little. The only alternative they have to acquire power is to organize the community, and this they are doing all over the nation. They will be heard, soon.

PHONY VS. AUTHENTIC

Another characteristic which seems to run throughout the new generation is the ability to *spot a phony*. Young adults are able to distinguish between the sincere and the insincere, the haughty and the humble, the pompous and the genuine, those who talk down and those who come to them as equals, the fuzzy-minded and the open-minded. They are more quickly turned off by a phony than by any other sort of person. They can accept adults—yes, even adults—if

47

they come willing to expose themselves and seek to learn together what is happening today.

MOVEMENTS VS. ESTABLISHMENTS

The movements are gaining a broader base of support and sympathy. By movements I am referring to organizations such as Students for Democratic Society (SDS), the Student Nonviolent Coordinating Committee (SNCC), the New Left (political posture), the Free Speech Movement, the Peace Movement, the Society for Individual Rights (SIR), and smaller, local movements to teach pride to Negroes or institute reforms in welfare services or revise the assumptions about higher education (Free University) or educate the public about sexual variations or organize the homosexual community or organize the poor to run their own communities. These are the great spritual movements now spreading throughout the United States, and in most cases around the world.

This interest in the movements needs to be examined with some care, for it would appear on the surface that with all the movement people rounded together we are still dealing with no more than 20 percent of the new generation. I believe the figure is fairly accurate. But what that kind of tallying does not indicate is the kind of sympathy that exists from other new generation people who in no way maintain a formal affiliation with the movements, nor would they ever do so. The estimates run high in this category, but there is as yet no research which can provide an accurate figure. Best estimates are that as many as 50 to 80 percent of the remainder of the new generation will at times or regularly indicate sympathetic support for the concerns of the movements in opposition to the Establishment. What is important here is to recognize that, though the statistic is not precise, the trend is clear.

Even more important to identify is the fact that the movements formulate the anti-Establishment feelings and attitudes of the generation and in so doing have been able to get this broader though reserved support. This support shows up in a variety of ways. In the civil rights effort of one southern city the concentration centered on a local cafeteria. Sip-ins were conducted by supporting whites in an effort to emphasize the pressure which had been building through several consecutive days of street demonstrations. Word of the sip-in filtered back to a group of young adults, none of whom ever had actively taken (and, I predict, never will take) a position in a sip-in or a demonstration. But, as I listened to this group discussing the issue, it became increasingly clear that the majority sympathized with their peers, even though they were definitely unwilling to "go help out." Those few in the group who took a strong position criticizing the demonstrations, and the sip-in in particular, suddenly found themselves on a defensive side, being bombarded by all types of subtle questions which revealed a kind of support for the right of others to try to improve a bad situation.

So as long as the movements form around issues and focus against the Establishment in one form or another, we can expect that, when the chips are down, the majority of the current new generation will stand with the movements rather than with the Establishment. It is just too

49

much to expect that they are going to give that much support to the Establishment. There is increasing evidence that the influence of the movements is already making progress in forcing the redefinition of an acceptable Establishment posture.

three

I Don't Like Church

Let me tell you the main reason I don't attend any more, or at least not regularly. Since leaving home to go out on my own, I've visited all kinds of churches, but they all seem just about the same. All of them strike me as being about as enervating as a cup of lukewarm postum. When I do go to church, what do I hear? From the pulpit, a semi-religious version of what Kenneth Galbraith calls "the conventional wisdom." From the choir loft, incredible Victorian anthems—"the kind that Grandma used to love." From the pew, the attitude you discover at alumni reunions—"where there's not a single dry eye but nobody believes a word of it." And from the boutonniered ushers, the kind of mechanical handshake which makes me suspect that they would greet Jesus at the Second Coming by saying: "It was nice of you to come."

In short, Pastor, the average church stands as a perfect symbol of nearly everything I despise—false gentility, empty sentiment, emotional impoverishment, intellectual mediocrity, and spiritual tepidity. Maybe it's my pride speaking, but I just don't want to be identified with an institution like that. Why is it that the modern church seems to have taken as its model the church at Laodicea? [1]

Sound too strong? The author of this statement wrote, "The point of view is pretty strong. . . . I feel the attitudes expressed are quite representative of the attitudes of many articulate young adults." [2]

I have used this "Memo" by Larson often. I have found only one church young adult group in which the majority felt that it did not represent the way they feel. The vocabulary and sources go beyond the unsophisticated young adult. The attitudes in the "Memo" permeate the generation.

There is a universality of spirit among the new generation, manifesting itself around the globe. A young adult in England says,

Religion to most (of us) . . . is an old person's fairy-tale . . . The Church has no meaning—a place full of old ladies in felt hats and smelling of cats and Pekinese. Boring sermons, meaningless prayers.

Everything they see around them is completely irreligious. Being "expected" to believe in God is ridiculous. Religion is for old people who have given up living and so need this fantasy about better life hereafter. It's not for young people who want to live, explore, find out about life themselves. [3]

Many people in the new generation have tried the church. They know more about it than we realize. Their absence from the church is the end product of a serious search. They seek a message of meaning and "good news" for their own day-to-day life experiences. More young people leave the church in search of truth than in rebellion against its authoritarian style. Both causes contribute to a gap between the church and the new generation.

A young man in a southern city had attended the worship service of a nearby church. He summarized his experience with the words, "No good news today!" Let's face the truth: he is not atypical, he is the typical young man or woman in our society today.

You say, "We have young adults in our church," and I reply, "I know that. But we both know the church as an institution is viewed by the large rank and file of the new generation as irrelevant, unnecessary, callous, afraid, and terribly self-centered."

OPINIONS ABOUT THE CHURCH

"No Church Wants Me!" A few years ago in one of our large cities I went with friends to hear a local entertainer. Between shows the entertainer came to our table. I was introduced as a clergyman. The entertainer turned to me and without one moment's hesitation he said, "I grew up in a Methodist church. You see me here as I really am. Tell me which church in this city would like to have me!" I could only reply honestly: so far as I knew or could imagine, he would not be welcome in any church. He accepted the answer but added, "You're right; no church wants me!"

The entertainer was a male homosexual who was a very good professional entertainer doing female impersonations. He had been an officer in his church youth program. He still wanted to attend church occasionally, if not regularly. He had tried attending anonymously. It was hollow, phony.

How could he bring his real life under review through the worship experience if he could only attend by concealing his identity? He was correct. No church wanted him if he was determined that he would come as he was, revealing his real identity. The church may not be for saints only, but somehow it seldom sees itself for this kind of person. Every major city has a large and massive population of rejected, disadvantaged people who are not welcome in most churches. Much of that population is young adult. Many, like the entertainer I met, are sure that no church wants them. They know that the modern church is generally unwilling to demonstrate that people are worth loving, regardless of their station or situation in life. And many straight, typical young adults, seeing the church silently and carefully turn its back on people in trouble, have concluded, "If the church doesn't care about them, the church can go to hell!"

Happiness Is Being in the Church! A few years ago I conducted some depth examinations of church young adult groups. One attitude seemed to be held by the leaders in every group. It was a feeling that meeting in the name of this church group was better than meeting under any other "flag."

They found some way to do everything they wanted to do under the name of the church. If it was dancing, the church had a dance. If swimming, the church had a swim party. If skiing, the church had a ski retreat. If talking about marriage, the church group met to talk about marriage. If they wanted to serve someone, the church took on a service project. The pattern was always the same.

It became clear that these young adults see the church

as a "safe" place where they can live without having to meet people who are different. They were incapable of associating with the larger new generation life style. For them happiness was being in the church, either group or building, but preferably both.

The irony is that these are the ones most likely to go into church professions. They are most often held up as "model" young churchmen. But they are not. They are incapable of loving the world—they fear life. They are hiding in the church. They don't give a damn for what we call the ministry of the laity in the world. Their style is to use the church as an escape from the world. The high endorsement of these as model young churchmen is inexcusable on theological and biblical grounds. But literally thousands of clergy, both pastors and connectional leaders who are more interested in religious institutions than Christian faith, daily assure this type of young person that his mere presence at the church is a genuine Christian act.

I do not want to be interpreted as feeling that these persons should not be welcomed in our church groups. Their condition clearly demands our response. But they need to be helped. They lack any adequate identity. They lack faith and hope and love. The church's ministry to these people must be more than giving them a group of people, each one clinging to another, even as helpful as that may appear. When the leadership core is made up of these persons, more mature, self-confident young men and women visit the group and are rather quickly repulsed from such a situation. These are often looking for more mature approaches to Christian study or ways to put their beliefs into action.

In a few rare instances the more mature young adults

have seen the need to stay in these groups and attempt some ministry to the more dependent leadership core. Without taking over, they help the dependent members to work more specifically on their identity needs. They try to broaden the range and deepen the quality of the total group experience. But this is, indeed, a rare situation.

A Dead End Street to Nowhereville! "Church groups and church attendance," she said, "are just like the aisle of the church itself; they are dead end streets to nowhereville!" So this young girl at a church retreat summed up an attitude held by a great number of the active young adult population. They are looking for the action, but it "can't be found by going through a church group. It doesn't have access to the action." Churches are viewed as sterile, self-centered groups spending their energy in group maintenance efforts and occasionally in maintenance efforts for the larger congregation or denomination. They have narrowed the concept of Christian service until it is now church service. The great serving needs of the community never are on their lists of needed volunteers.

The action is in the community and the larger world today. The activist segment of the young adult world is going to be where the action is. If they can't get there through the church, they will go another route. What blocks access to the action becomes a block to their goals.

When church groups only *discuss* the civil rights movement and never join forces with others to demonstrate, they become dead ends. When they discuss the war in Vietnam and cannot make public their opinions about it, they are dead ends. When they discuss corruption in community life and go no further, they are dead ends. When they evaluate the church's worship as leaving them empty but can't confront the minister, they are dead ends. When they talk about human suffering and the compassion of God and never visit a jail or a hospital or the ghetto areas, they have become dead ends. When they believe that eighteen-year-olds should have a vote and remain unorganized and silent, they have become dead ends.

I Don't Like Church! This is the most prevalent attitude toward the church among the new generation. Many have discontinued regular association with the church. They have concluded they can do without it. They don't lay harsh condemnation on the church, nor do they come to her defense. They just live without it.

Many of them are members of a church, usually their parents' church. Membership never meant enough to have it transferred. Others transfer from city to city and denomination to denomination, trying to find a church that offers a vital experience. One young woman had been a member of seven churches, starting with the Primitive Baptist and including the Roman Catholic, Unitarian, Christian Science, and others. She had gradually moved westward from Iowa to San Diego. She had decided the "church bit" wasn't for her.

This attitude evaluates the church's educational efforts as mediocre, its music as sentimental, its preaching as pompous and irrelevant, and its understanding of and influence on life as nonexistent. Tragically, young adults do not expect the church to take stands in their behalf. The church is a phony. Its Word is buried in words, and its goals are for its own sake, not the welfare of all.

Where Was the Church When the Lights Went Out?
One attitude toward the church is disappointment and rejection. Young adults face numerous personal problems:
finances, parents, vocation, love, sex, marriage, drugs,
arrest, physical and mental health, the draft, among others.
For too many the church seems to be absent when needed.
Many have sought help but received criticism for expressing
doubts.

Others have taken their stand in the ranks of the civil
rights movement. They found a few churchmen there, but,
when they went home to ask what their local church or
clergy would do, they spoke to deaf ears and cold shoulders.
These people are not antichurch. But they know the church
is not fulfilling its intended purpose or its repeated
promises. They are among the people who responded with
affirmative nods to a recent cartoon in *Playboy*, portraying
a stuffy layman saying, "Frankly, doctor, don't you think
it's time to get off this civil rights kick and get back to the
fundamental teachings of Christianity?" They have expected great things of the church and have been
disappointed.

THE NEW GENERATION IN THE CHURCH

In the new generation there are a few who stay reason-
ably close to and visibly identified with the church. They
divide themselves into two groups with little in common.

The Young Churchmen. The larger of the two groups is
what I call young churchmen. They are concerned about
the things of the church. They are loyal to the practices and
expectations of "religion" as Bonhoeffer uses the word.
Their goal is to be good members of a church, that is, attend

regularly, be loyal, seek new recruits, make the church bigger and better. They are *not* interested in taking steps or actions which might possibly put the church in a "bad" light with anyone—regardless of Christian teaching to the contrary.

One recent misuse of my time took me to the annual meeting of Men's Work Secretaries. These are the bureaucrats who maintain "men's work" programs in the churches. The emphasis was on the young adult population. One morning a panel of three young churchmen spoke to us. One was a part-time employee of a denominational campus ministry program. Another was planning on a church career. The third was an officer in a campus religious group.

What these three represented and what they said was the voice of a decreasing minority group in the new generation. At most they might have represented 15 percent of the young population; a figure that high could only occur in the South, certainly not the East or West.

This new generation minority called young churchmen includes both young laymen and young professionals. No adequate studies have been made of them. However, in several isolated samples they reveal similar characteristics. The groups tested with the Rokeach Dogmatism Scale have all indicated high dogmatic characteristics. With these data and observation of many of these groups, one can conclude that these young churchmen are basically dependent individuals, relying heavily on external authoritarian sources for standards of behavior and belief. They are anxious, quick to conform, and eager to have adult "authorities" make policy decisions and exact expectations of conformity upon them.

Simply put, the truth is that these people need the church. They want to be told what is right and wrong, good and bad, moral and immoral. They want black and white guidelines. They want someone to tell them what constitutes a loyal member, a good churchman, a good boy or girl. Their basic personal makeup drives them to do as 'Simon says."

I suspect that at this point the reader is thinking, "This description doesn't fit the group of young adults at *my* church." Before you dismiss this description, I give you two facts. (1) Every church staff person or pastor who has been exposed to this description of his young generation people has believed his group to be an exception. (2) To my knowledge *every* church group tested with the Rokeach Dogmatism Scale has scored more dogmatic than the average score nationally and *does* reflect the above characteristics.

These people are willing to sing in choirs, serve as ushers, teach in Sunday schools, hold offices in young adult, women's, or men's groups, counsel youth groups, serve on committees, or almost anything else. They will stay very active in doing church things so long as someone keeps suggesting or approving the idea.

They will not tolerate much conflict or controversy. If newcomers are seeking controversy, they are apt to be given the old silent treatment. If "programs" touch on controversial issues, they are most often led by a group member who talks *about* the problems. Actively participating on one side or other of a local controversy is almost unheard of. It requires personal judgment and personal risk which con-

flict with the opinions of authority figures, and few are able
to venture out on their own against the real or imagined
adult expectations.

Fortunately, there are individual exceptions here and
there. But life in the church is a hard road for them.

The Young Secular Christians. This person is radically
different. He may or may not relate regularly to a local
established congregation. He will seldom be active in things
like young adult, men's, or women's groups. He will often
not have time for church activities, preferring to involve
himself in various service, social, reform, and protest efforts
on the critical issues of his city, nation, or world. This
young person is radically different. He is the lay man or
woman or the young clergyman who has tasted the food
of the renewal movement. His theological fathers are Bonhoeffer, Ogden, Niebuhr, Tillich, Barth. He has heard Rob-
inson, Pike, Mathews and Egan, and he hopes the church is
being radically renewed. He believes that the church as it is
usually present is inadequate to fulfill the Christian mission
in this later third of the twentieth century. He is akin in
spirit to Webber, Cox, Winter, Hargraves, Cosby, Benedict,
King, Durham, Colin Williams, Woodard, Alinsky. He is
concerned about secular ecumenism, about the world, about
meeting power with power, about a public faith and involvement in the world through radical love. He is not
particularly loyal to programs and goals of traditional
efforts of the church. Sometimes he is mistakenly seen as
anti-institutional. But he does not oppose organization or
even institutions. He does oppose investing himself in institutions which are reluctant to enter into the changes and
issues coming on the wings of the freedom revolution. He is

committed to serious study of cultural issues, self-aware-
ness, Christian freedom, corporate mission manifested in a
variety of ways in local situations. He is bound to others
by modes of celebrations, a somewhat distinctive vocabulary and a life style of participation in contemporary life.
Worthy of his attention are the critical issues affecting
human beings today: housing, welfare, health, government,
education, community organization, democracy, war, freedom and rights, individual dignity, faithfulness, and interdependence. He is one of the people Allan Brockway refers
to as "Secular Saints." Brockway contributes what he suggests is "A Creed for the Secular Saint" to which most of
these secular Christians would affirm.

> I trust myself to the absolute limits and impossible demands
> that define my life and call me to live its full definition; and
> commit myself to the reception and declaration of the possibility
> of life's goodness and death's goodness that is presented for
> my choosing from outside my consciousness and remains ex-
> ternal in my history as a constant possibility;
> And I gratefully embody my decision for self affirmation,
> number myself among those who live the free life; know I am
> significant; and hope ever to be momentarily renewed in this
> trust, in the sure awareness that my self is important throughout
> time.[4]

The secular Christian is found both in the institutional
church and outside it. His numbers are increasing. His
influence slowly affects denominations or orders of the
churches. This "renewal" movement is the shape of the
church of tomorrow, already breaking into our own reality.
It increases in strength and effectiveness across the nation
and world. Those in it are closer to one another than to

brother denominationalists. The Ecumenical Institute, through its unique methodology, is making one of the most significant Christian contributions being made to the world today. It is enabling young Christians to grasp an adequate view of the church in the world, going beyond understanding, to demonstrate effectively that concept of mission. It and the Southern Christian Leadership Conference are the most significant demonstrations of Christians as lovers of the world that exist in our time in the nation. To these one could add recognition to the long-established East Harlem Protestant Parish and the new model in the Glide Urban Center in San Francisco.

_____ *four*

*Views on the State of the Church*_____

"Today's Church may be standing at a fateful crossroads in her history—unable to resurrect traditions of the past and likewise unable to sense the Judgment implied by her present irrelevance to the world." So writes Howard Moody from his perspective as pastor-director of an experimental congregation in New York City and a member of the North American Working Party exploring the World Council of Churches priority concern, the missionary structure of the congregation.

Mr. Moody is not alone. The church has arrived at a point when it has only the faintest idea what it is or what it is to be in the immediate world of tomorrow. We are facing the crisis of our own identity. The Rev. Dr. Gordon Cosby, minister of Washington's well-known Church of the

Saviour, says, "We are going to have to give up the myth of Christendom because there is no longer any Christendom. It does not exist in the sense in which we have always thought of it. The population explosion is so great that the birth rate far exceeds the conversion rate."

GOING OUT OF BUSINESS

The church is a declining institution. Try as we can, there is no way to conclude that the church is a thriving, growing, expanding, highly influential institution in contemporary society or culture. That is true both in the local situation and in the national picture as well.

During the last three decades Christendom has experienced nothing less than a shaking of its foundations. . . .

The Christian community today is a diminishing minority. The number of confessing Christians in the Western countries has dimished considerably in recent years. The spread of communism in Eastern Europe and China has resulted in a decrease of church membership [there also]. The missionary advance in many of the Asian countries has been halted and even reversed. The fast rate of growth of population among predominantly non-Christian peoples of Asia, who account for half of the world's population, has increased the proportion of non-Christians in the world as a whole.

In such a situation it is hard to believe that history is moving towards the Christian hope that "every tongue (shall) confess that Jesus Christ is Lord, to the glory of God the Father" (Phil. 2:11).[1]

In the United States the membership explosion of the 1950's has not slackened; it has ended. Churches, with the exception of the smaller evangelical and pentecostal bodies, have ceased not only to maintain growth in proportion to the population growth; they have actually begun to show statistical net losses of members, constituents, dollars, leadership, and so forth. This is not a sudden and temporary reversal either. It has come on gradually. Beginning with slight declines in the growth rate, it now shows clear losses.

I find this a reason for serious reflection. I do not find it a cause for fear, for loss of faith, or for stopgap efforts. I happen to believe that the church is a gift, an inheritance of mankind, and that its spirit will be manifested throughout human history. Its forms will change as its calling or functions are adapted to the events and priorities of the emerging history.

This emergent history is now calling for a priority to deal with the increasing absence of members of the new generation from the active life of the church. Though large numbers are on the membership rolls of churches somewhere, they are increasingly inactive, cut off from and indifferent about the church. They have not found it to be a needed or worthwhile association for friendships, information, counsel, or involvement in the crucial issues of these days.

Mankind is discovering means of communication and transportation which draw us nearer and nearer to the time when we may be able to have a worldwide spirit of community, and hopefully unity, among men and nations. William Coffin has said that "a unified mankind is *the* great revolutionary fact of our time." Simultaneously we are experiencing "trouble" in maintaining a sense of unity with our own sons and daughters.

So the church is first and foremost under attack from the young themselves. Second, it is under attack from many of the institutions of our day. Some of these institutions compete for the loyalty, time, and money of the young for causes which range from the profit motive to the ideals offered in the Peace Corps to the black power advocates.

Another attack comes on the church today from theological quarters. This attack says simply that to segment the church and place young adults or youth or any other part of the full membership of the church in a separated relationship with less than full rights and full authority is destructive of the unity which the church is seeking for mankind.

WHO'S AT THE CONTROLS?

Younger members feel excluded from much of the total life and effort of the church. They know that the older members of the church feel that they can run the church faithfully and properly without the counsel or concerns of the young.

We have too long encouraged young people to think of the church as a place where they are "educated" and entertained rather than as a place where they are involved in the mutual ministries of a priesthood of all believers. The young are put out into marginal activities and told to run their own operations. They are told under what conditions and within what limits they may act as the church or in the name of the church.

In 99 cases out of 100 the church provides [them] with communities which require feelings of duty, loyalty and obedience rather than joy, partnership and belonging. In the words of one of them: "In my home church they isolate the Gospel from the world and assimilate it to their group!" [2]

What happens is that, even when the younger adults

67

attempt to remain faithful to the church, they find that they are not fully included. They have discovered that, while the church claims to be different from other organizations, in practice it uses the same standards to make decisions as do secular organizations. Churchmen select leaders on the basis of age, wealth, position, or "company" loyalty instead of trying to create a way for all to exercise a voice. They set goals which increase the status and place of the church in the community without much regard for the great sins and immoralities evident in the city. They collect and disburse great amounts of funds only where they can have control or can spend the money in their own self-interest, such as for buildings. They contend that they are acting in behalf of the whole without seeking opinions or support from younger members.

All paternalism on the part of the church toward young people [young adults] should now be seen for the inexcusable error that it is. Young people are not "the future of the church." That sentiment can be regarded as true only by those who think in purely institutional terms. . . . [They] *are* the church now in their sector of the world's life and should accordingly be fully integrated into the life of the churches.[3]

Control of the church is exercised primarily at levels of our life beyond the local congregation. Board secretaries, bishops, bureaucrats, presiding leaders, and clerks hold great power and influence. True, local churches do have a kind of autonomy, but they are associated with a denomination or other grouping from which they receive much of the information on which they base their decisions. These larger organizations call for a kind of overarching loyalty. "The church is bigger than any one congregation" (especially if it does something of which others or the hierarchy disapproves). This larger organization takes on all the signs of authority through titles, prestige, status, visibility, centralization, money management, and goal setting. This is true whether the label is association or conference or synod or diocese or whatever. The amount of authority finally exercised from "above" depends on the persons placed in these positions and their ideology and personal needs. These persons are almost always older adults; they are seldom, if ever, young adults.

On both local and regional levels the church is generally under the primary influence of the professional churchmen. The clergy, the professional educators, musicians, managers, yes, and secretaries exercise the greatest influence in determining not only decisions but, even more important, *what issues will be raised* for consideration and decision. This must not be viewed as solely negative. The reason we have professionals is to provide primary leadership. But a danger is present when for whatever reason the balance of authority between the membership and the professionals becomes ineffective as a basis for arriving at commonly held goals.

There is today a widespread recognition that the professionals are "in control." The danger is that, if this continues to be true, the price will be a serious erosion of the concern, judgment, and perspectives of the general membership. This problem has reached crisis dimensions. Local leadership in many churches rests almost entirely on what the professionals counsel. When such counsel is accepted, experience is showing that there results a widening misunderstanding about the rationale, *the reason* for specific efforts. Add to this confusion the deliberate efforts of the right-wing, pseudoreligious, extremist groups to create unrest in the churches, and we are sure to have a mass desertion or a revolution on our hands. The current signs point to a desertion. In many churches the most socially aware and involved adults have begun to decline places of leadership, for they cannot get support for their ideas. The professional continues to appease the angry members rather than give a significant demonstration of what it means to be a Christian man or woman in today's world. This cowardice of the professional is the pivotal link in the present decline of the church. The conservatives have learned that one of the weaknesses of the piety most professionals hold is that they cannot tolerate persons being angry with them. Thus open anger becomes a tool of the conservatives to produce conformity and conservatism in the professional. Intimidated clergy repeatedly counsel toward caution and the avoidance of controversial issues.

There are many young adults among the professionals. They are of two kinds. One group are what Roy Larson calls the "young fogies." They do not belong to the new generation. They have adopted the ideas, the perceptions, the attitudes, and the loyalties of the older generation. They belong—head, heart, and hands—to the institution which is run by and for the adult culture.

The other group is the vocal and visible young professionals, questioning, challenging, changing the institution—its ways, its forms, its style, its image—as much as they possibly can. They are the young clergy who are often in "trouble" with the institution. They are the legions who after five to ten years (or more) withdraw, feeling that the institution just can't move into the modern world with a spirit of service.

AN ESTABLISHMENT SCENT

The church seems clearly to be recognized as a part of the enemy of the young generation—the Establishment. If the church is an Establishment institution, it has indeed failed. If it is even perceived as such, it has failed to communicate or demonstrate its intended, or true, identity and purpose. Like it or not, we are viewed this way. The church is a status quo institution, and to find evidence one has only to look at its negligence to take significant leadership in the search for peace or the fight for civil rights or the reforms of unjust laws or the exposing of evil and immoral practices in our culture. Strange as it may seem, the general populace expects a great deal from the church. The present leadership of the church, at every level, seems too content to view the church as a *container* rather than an actor, or, more biblically accurate, a transformer. We are hobbyists in today's revolutionary world, collecting names, bricks, dollars, and acres while reading piles and piles of our own publications and discussing them with one another.

This conservatism characterizes almost everything we do with the new generation. When the new generation turned out to man the civil rights movement, we gathered in sanctuaries to discuss the pros and cons of civil disobedience. When they rallied to pick up the Meredith march and needed food, health care, and other support on the long march, we met to cover our fear or disinterest with talk of the "split" in the Negro movement. Here and there, a few individuals went to be on the line. "In more churches than we would like to concede, committed Christianity is equated with faithful attendance in the parish youth group. We speak about 'uncommitted young people' and mean simply that they do not belong to any of *our* organizations for them!" [4]

Under present leadership, involvement has come to be defined in terms of participation in church activities. The professionals are constantly heard from pulpit, lectern, and periodicals, advocating that members give more support to church activities and, if necessary, give up some of the involvements they have in the community. One pastor of a church where I worshiped actually declared that true renewal would come to that church when we gave more money and had more Sunday school teachers! When this kind of theology is allowed to continue without correction from other professionals, then we accept privatism, in its most divisive and deadly form, as a normative posture for the church today. That privatism, the withdrawal from men of all conditions, is the beginning of failure and disobedience and unfaithfulness. If the church is ever to be seen as an institution of integrity and worth by the new generation, it must demonstrate a public concern for the whole of mankind. It must show that concern we call "good news," namely, that God demonstrated his love for all men through being present with us. And it must do so *in kind*. No amount of talk or status will substitute. Those who are willing to undertake this demonstration must take control of the church.

VANISHING IDENTITY

The crisis of identity is a crisis of national proportions and spreads throughout both the personal and institutional life of this nation. This crisis permeates the entire life of the church. The basic question of "Who am I?" or "Who are we?" is being raised with increasing frequency and, fortunately, with more openness and less caution or reservations than even five years ago. I say *fortunately* because I believe that, unless the church can discover and become aware of its own identity and nature, it will become an even more and more irrelevant institution. It could become a gross burden and detriment to contemporary human communities, whether associated for religious, productive, commercial, recreational, planning, or learning purposes. Whether we like it or not, the church as a body cannot give a clear and comprehensible answer to the question, "Who or what are you?" No doubt there will be, from many quarters, an audible answer; but the meaning and consequence of such answers have not, in my experience, hit the eardrums (to say nothing of the spirit) of the hearers as the sounds of "good news." Let's face the truth: most such replies have about the same effect on the hearer as Littlechap's political speeches from the stage play *Stop the World —I Want to Get Off*. One petty speech he makes begins with the words

> Mumbo jumbo
> Rhubarb rhubarb
> Tickety bubarb
> Yak yak yak.
> Mumbo jumbo

73

Red white and bluebarb
Poor Britannia's on her back.*

BASIS OF FORMER IDENTITY

The problem of identity relates to the change occurring today. But, specifically, the goals which for so long gave the church its reason for being and its self-identity are no longer acceptable. They are outgrown. The question of identity is closely tied into the discussion of the revolution in matters of piety. For many years our identity and purpose were based on a few basic positions.

First, the doctrine of God's action which dominated our thinking, planning, and actions was that God relied solely on the church to communicate his word, good news, and judgment to the world (generally phrased "the rest of the world"). This assumption clearly proceeded on the principle that the church was God's mouthpiece. When it spoke, God was heard; when it was silent, God had not exerted his will or desire into the matter. It was as if there were a clause in the historic covenant guaranteeing that the church would at least receive advance notice of God's action or intention and in most matters the church would be his exclusive spokesman.

If that were ever true, I'm afraid that recent times have clearly shown that God forgot to read the small print in the contract. Wherever a spirit of truth and love have been needed, God has raised up someone to provide the leader-

---

* "Mumbo Jumbo" From the musical production *Stop the World —I Want to Get Off*. Words and Music by Leslie Bricusse and Anthony Newley TRO © Copyright 1961 Essex Music Ltd., London, England. All Publication Rights Controlled by Ludlow Music, Inc., New York, for the U.S.A. and Canada. Used by permission.

ship. And it has not always been from within the church. How frustrating this is for those who even yet hold to the old view. But our present history teaches us that we do not hold exclusive rights to speak for God, nor to organize men to act in keeping with his will.

Second, the church seemed to get itself well implanted in relationship to the doctrines of God's grace. With the hardening of one or more forms of the sacrament—a form to recall and celebrate that God is a God of grace—the church became the *sole dispenser* of God's grace. It was as if again it held exclusive distributorship of his grace. Where, when, to whom, and how it should be administered were decisions of the church. The church seemed to take the liberty to set the retail price. For example, in certain churches grace simply wasn't available to people unless their skin was white. In other churches it was available only on proof of membership in the "club." These lesser prerequisites become the criteria for admission and were often given more importance than the intentions of the person seeking grace. They have, both in fact and in practice, governed and determined who have been recipients of the elements of the celebration of his *ever-present* grace.

The idea that grace is dependent on anything except the desire for forgiveness and the recipient's acceptance is foolish and presumptuous thinking. The idea that a celebration of the merciful spirit of God can make first- and second-class Christians at any time or place is an absurdity. Today those who form the underground church around the world practice the corporate celebration without regard to these lesser things. It seems apparent that the gift of grace

75

comes on the wings of love, whether the proper silver, brass, or wooden fixtures or words are present or not.

Third, the church assumed a relationship to the non-church world which set church and world in opposition to each other. The goal of the church was to get all men into its membership, or at least constituency, by calling on them to renounce the world and its so-called temptations. The world became a hunting ground into which Christians went only reluctantly in order to find a way to support their families. Basically the world was bad. It was as if somehow the church actually believed that person-by-person, dollar-by-dollar, and acre-by-acre it was gradually going to incorporate the entire world out of the worldly environment and into the churchly sphere. The "really faithful layman" became the one who was there every time the doors opened and held from six to twenty positions in the church's organizational life. Neither motivation nor competency was to be compared to willingness.

To capture and baptize the world as Christians with the brand of the cross is an unreal and distorted goal for the contemporary church. The goal of the church is to continue the presence of Jesus' spirit in the midst of all mankind. It is a witness we must perform, not a conquest. Jesus gave to men according to their needs. That is our goal: to see that men receive from this world's resources according to their needs. Jesus demonstrated a life of love and care, and he didn't seem to think it made much difference in whose name it was done, so long as it was done. Ever since apostolic times there has been an element in the church who has tried to make us an exclusive group primarily concerned for God and one another, with only a marginal concern for the whole of mankind.

Fourth, the objective of leaders and members alike was to have a church so set up (theologically it proved to be *up-set*) that every member had a job to do in the church. That job became one's *church work!* This is still a widely held view of the nature of the work of the church. But it is wrong—theologically and biblically. It is an evasion of the more important nature of the church's work and mission. *The work of the church is in the world.* It is here that our faithfulness and our obedience are tested and measured. The work of the laity is not *at* nor *in* the church (either building or group) but in his own vocation, his own associations, his own neighborhood, and in the daily events of his own life.

With the outgrowth of these four presuppositions about the work and identity of the church, it should be no surprise that an identity crisis is upon us. All four of these principles are now too small, too narrow to stand the tide of renewed biblical study, concerted theological reflection, and the wisdom of recent practice and consequences. These must be discarded. (It should be noted that, though this view of the church is changing, there are places where the possibility of change has caused segments of the church to hold even more firmly to the old propositions.) One of my old-fashioned friends once advised that, if a sermon had a weak point, it should be delivered louder and more aggressively in order to keep anyone from raising a question about it. Some folks, seeing the weaknesses in the old propositions, only try to bolster them up—but they are obsolete, and they are passing out as our frame of reference.

AN INDIVIDUAL MATTER

This crisis of our own identity exists as an individual and personal matter. It is personal because individual members of the church have no clearly identifiable understanding or image of what it means to be a Christian. The average Christian person can provide some generalized slogans in answer to the question, "What is a Christian today?" The replies are apt to be "Being a Christian is a seven-day-a-week job; it's not just a person with Sunday religion" or "Being a Christian means loving God and your neighbor(s)" or "Being a Christian means putting others first" or some other oversimplified equation which means something quite different to each person who formulates it for an answer and still different things to those who hear it.

What does a Christian do and why? Being a Christian today is a complex affair, and simple formulas are more apt to be traps or evasions than adequate understandings. One reason many new generation people have little use for us is that many Christians oversimplify contemporary life and its complex moral and ethical issues.

To be a Christian today has been the subject of endless discussions, sermons, papers, and several books. Related to the question is the doctrine of man. Christians can only be men (or women). They cannot be angels. Being a Christian, then, has to do with being human. The highest goal any human can attempt to achieve through his system of beliefs and the piety he exercises is to be a human being living life to its fullest meaning and worth. The Christian life is then a style of living that relates immediately and significantly to the life one has on earth. It is a life style which can be attempted by ordinary men and also by extraordinary men. It is a life which is conditioned to exercise a sense of compassion tempered with a concern for the welfare of both the individual and the larger society. At the same time it is also conditioned to offer the cup of water without conditions or demands. It is a life of simple concern and response, and it is a life of complex ethical considerations and relatively selected responses. It is a life exercising a quality referred to as love, demonstrating a characteristic known as hope, and motivated and reinforced by an abstract element called faith.

And individual Christians can take such concepts and statements as these or a thousand similar attempts and live meaning into them. It is not uncommon today to find people equating the Christian life with certain forms created to demonstrate the Christian life in another era. Today the identity of a Christian is not based on absolute actions, but on an evaluation of each problem as it arises and a relative response within the range of what seems appropriate.

AN INSTITUTIONAL CRISIS

Though the roots of the Christian identity lie in the understanding within individual Christian persons, it is too simple to view that as the total problem. The institutional church must also share in the diffusion of identity and the subsequent crisis.

The church as an institution has a responsibility to formulate what is an adequate understanding of the identity of Christians both individually and corporately. That formulation must also be enacted thrugh some kind of visible and distinguishable demonstration or model of what such a meaning implies in practice and behaviors. It must ac-

79

knowledge those who attempt this demonstration with clear support.

But the identity question arises as often and as elusively in the gathered church seeking a way to witness as elsewhere. What is the church? And what is she called to be and do, today? Significant breakthroughs have come on this matter in a few isolated situations. In the East Harlem Protestant Parish, the Church of the Saviour, and several other congregations and groups, Christians are working to clarify their own identity and to formulate new pietistic forms to enact what they have come to believe. In the East Harlem Parish they came to believe that the church must have greater influence on the kind of thinking done in all kinds of community organizations and groups. So one of the disciplines of the parish was that every member must also join one community group and work conscientiously within it to accomplish what might be called Christian objectives. These objectives were to be formulated in such a way as to be the best possible solution to one of the difficult problems of the East Harlem area. In the Church of the Saviour the people felt that there must be something of a very specific and tangible nature to which God was calling or would call them. But there was no specific clarity or agreement. After months of Bible study and searching for a clear call or sense of mission, they agreed that they were being called to get in dialogue with the world. So the Potter's House, one of the very first and most significant coffeehouses run by a church, was planned and opened. The church members staff it and deliberately get into dialogue with those who come in. Because of this dialogue with others, similar study groups continue to find clear directions to which they must give themselves: for example, a creative arts workshop, a farm-type retreat center, house churches, a factory.

The number of church groups who have tried to short-cut the personal and group searching process and simply infiltrate community groups or coffeehouses or some other form which came through serious seeking and obedience is legion. And their failures are also legion. The clue is that one must find his sense of mission through serious reflection, study, and involvement with the general community or group which seems to be the context of one's ministry. If we are to work with young adults, what is to be done is going to come only through being with, listening to, and probing the minds of the people of the new generation. An adequate sense of mission seldom comes in any other way, though I would not want to standardize this process.

TEMPTATIONS TO TINKER

With the identity crisis before us we must be aware that the roots of it are deep in moral and ethical concerns about what the church is to be in the midst of the human world. And, as with almost all ethical questions which have arisen in the past decade and a half in America, we are not facing it squarely. Instead, we are attempting to round off the corners, soften the center, and propose some technological or organizational "way out." Which is not a way out of the dilemma but a way of avoiding it. It is a sheer escape device. And that is exactly what is now occurring in the church.

Having discovered the crisis is upon us in ways that can no longer be ignored, we have started to look for solutions by *tinkering*. We will do all kinds of tinkering with our past in a pretense that somewhere back there we can find the point at which we turned left and should have turned right. If we are lost, there simply must be a reason; and, if we can find the reason that lies in our past, then all can be corrected. But fortunately churches are not assembly lines, and it is not easy to retrace our history. Nor is it much use to try to change the past. But we do try, and we invest hours and dollars in the attempt.

In addition to the past, we also play an even more popular game of tinkermanship: "change the parts." So one by one we take up the organs of the institution and examine them. If we identify flaws, we attempt to throw them out. Specifically, people today are doing this as they make all kinds of charges against publications, boards, bishops, young clergy, behavior, seminaries, the National Council of Churches, laity, etc. But it doesn't make any (or at least not much) difference. And we knew it all the time, for what we do is to put back all the same parts or substitute a reconditioned part vulnerable to the same so-called flaws. There have been too few efforts at reorganization which have been done on the premise that weak parts should be removed. I agree with a recent statement by a leader in the management field who suggested that executives of the next forty years must be men who can dismiss people who have become obsolete, either by sending them into a retraining program or by dismissing them completely. But the church does neither. We have turned something labeled a "call" into an idolatrous form, and we hide behind it rather than discipline one another.

FACING THE CRISIS

When the preceding information is examined alongside the kind of change and growth that has taken place in American life and culture in the past twenty years, one thing seems to be relatively clear. The identity problem is not a question of "lost identity" through some catastrophic event. Rather, the old identity has been outgrown, both by the culture and now by the church itself. This being the case, our hope is not in these tinkering processes. While there is room for considerable reexamination of the theological tradition of the church, *it is not some old identity which we are now called to find once again.* No, this is a new age, it is new wine, and the wineskin will be new also. This identity which we seek will come forth only in practice. It is to be discovered, invented, created, and accomplished through acts, not words; through faith-risk, taking in what some will label radical roles of obedience to Jesus' word and style.

Dr. C. I. Itty of the World Council of Churches was speaking correctly when he wrote,

> The influence of the Christian church in society and even among its own members is decreasing rapidly. . . . The emergence of welfare states in various countries has diminished the role of the church in education and welfare services. The local church is no longer the center of European village [or American community] as it was for centuries. The parish priest [or minister] is no longer the leader of the village community. . . . The church has little control over major decisions affecting the life of the men and society. History runs its course, bypassing the church.[5]

Dr. Itty has been insightful in noting that the church during the nineteenth century and early twentieth century expanded itself through heavy involvement in the fields of education and welfare services. The church was for a long time the major carrier of the cause of higher education. Then came the land-grant colleges. And after that the burst of tax support for education which, over a few decades, moved the church from primary carrier of the cause of higher education to a minority role in the field. The identical pattern has occurred with regard to welfare services. Housing, feeding, clothing, and health care for the poor are now the concern and responsibility of national, state, and local governments. The church, again, has become a small partner in this overwhelming enterprise. Each of these represents great victories for the church. A value it held has now become a value held by the culture at large.

The beginnings in education were motivated by our belief that the church must challenge man to attain his fullest self-discovery and thereby achieve the ability to make a significant contribution to the common good. To do this, men needed greater education. So the church established schools of higher education, first to produce this kind of man to fill the leadership needs of the church itself and, shortly after, to begin educating people for various professional fields, particularly teaching and law. Today our whole society has set an opportunity for higher education as a norm and essential aspect of our national life. The original need has been accomplished, namely, a way to provide the society with learned and informed men and women.

In the area of welfare services the church has, from its historic outset, taken collections for the welfare of others: widows, children, and the poor. This practice has been a primary reason for the existence of the church. The fact that in the twentieth century government has begun to take a major responsibility for the underprivileged is indeed the sign of success in our effort to declare that the world has enough for all and all deserve access to at least a minimal kind of subsistence. Now this aspect of provision is incorporated into the nation's policies, even though too often the compassion is lost before the benefit reaches the individual. The government does not intend to let people go hungry, naked, unhoused, or suffer or die unnecessarily.

These two illustrations serve to make the crucial point on the state of the church. The church, having seen its earlier goals become accepted and incorporated into the culture at large, suddenly finds itself without an adequate sense of direction for the immediate present and unable to regroup sufficiently to hear, discover, identify, describe, accept its calling in new directions. If we believe that God is always at work before us, then there is surely something to be done in this age which is equally as crucial as have been the causes of education and social welfare in past times.

SOMETHING TO DO—A CAUSE WORTH SOMETHING

Several years ago Father Robert Young, priest of the Protestant Episcopal Church and director of the Bishop Anderson House in the center of a gigantic medical complex of Chicago, spoke of the work which he and his associates did in this way. After explaining that the church present in the medical community must become involved in the community's life and then play the game of waiting, Father Young said,

Probably the one thing that has really gotten us into the medical center is being on the wards . . . , being involved. . . . I've learned . . . that it is absolutely important to have something to do. I have never walked through a hospital that I did not get involved with somebody. . . .

All week long our clergy are involved in personal conferences, teaching, and so forth.[6]

I think we find ourselves as the church in the situation of the village blacksmith of the 1920's. He had had a booming business. It appeared unlimited until the gasoline engine was mounted on a car or truck. The moment that happened, the future of all blacksmiths was affected radically. But their responses were quite varied. Some scoffed at machines. Some grew fearful and simply tried to hang on. Others realized that they had some skills and some assets to apply to the new day. They could work metal. They had shops and forges. Some took agencies and sold the "contraptions." Others went into the auto repair business. This is where we are in the church today. We are more like the middle group of blacksmiths—those who put off a decision and kept trying to hang on by respect and friendships earned from an earlier time. But time proved that, if they couldn't provide a contribution to the times, they just couldn't be afforded. So it is with us. We have been getting by on our reputation, our friends, and mystical products for the past few decades, and *time* is now beginning rapidly to close in on us.

People everywhere are deciding today that they cannot afford the luxury of generosity to their old friend, the church, any longer. Church budgets are going down as population goes up. People are giving less because they do not see clearly why they should be giving more. The appeal to building programs held us for two decades, but it is not going to be accepted as a reason to give much longer. More and more, nothing ultimately significant is happening in these buildings.

Something did happen when our fathers built colleges. Something did happen when they built hospitals, orphanages, collected for relief of the poor. The people, in general, believed that what they were doing was important, and they gave their loyalty and their money.

Another clear sign of reduced giving is the way in which young people give themselves to leadership as professionals. Fewer young men are going into the ministry and priesthood, even fewer staying in after the first decade.

The single most urgent business the church faces is the clarification of *a new major thrust worth the commitment* of a man's life—one so evident that it can unite men of goodwill and moral character into a thrust purposeful to communities again. But this cannot happen so long as the agencies and orders of the churches maintain the competitiveness of recent years. Somewhere there must come a task force of competence and faithfulness and vision sufficient to bring this new mission before us with clarity. Such efforts are imperative. The life of the contemporary institutional church is at stake. In every culture in every age, institutions sustaining religious goals and values only exist as long as people believe in their worth and meaningfulness. And the signs of this decade are fearfully clear.

The church must find new directions for itself which are ultimately for the whole of mankind—whether it be an extension of a present position such as working to provide every person with a minimum level of living, or a radically new goal such as establishing interdisciplinary centers for ethical considerations in every national and regional capital in the world and in all major metropolitan complexes, or aggressive work to teach citizens to live interracially in schools, businesses, neighborhoods, religious and social associations.

Whatever the nature of this new goal or direction, it must stand the test of the new generation—is it needed, critically needed? Is it something which can be accomplished eventually? Will the church have the courage to work to accomplish it in spite of opposition? What place will the new generation have in sharpening the problems and designing plans and making interim decisions?

The new generation is the fodder of Vietnam, the biggest loser of life in the urban riots, the chief "blood donors" in the civil rights movement. They will not join the church to be used as martyrs, victims, scapegoats, or for other "dirty" work only. If they believe in the goals, they will take the roles by their own choice. They will not go into many more of the Establishment's battles in which no one knows just what the objective is. Our objective must be made clear.

PARTNERSHIP WITH THE NEW GENERATION

No new directions will be adequately defined without the help of a considerable number of new generation people at the planning table with voice and vote. They have the most accurate perceptions of current reality. Not just any of them, and probably not the ones who are most numerous in our church groups, but the brightest of the new generation can and would contribute significantly to such an effort. One of the reasons our church is becoming so staid and so estranged from the young is that we have failed to recognize that *we need the perceptions of the young*. We don't need the young for democratic reasons nearly so much as we need their perspectives, their opinions, their experience in our continual planning. Almost without exception, the ages of members on any national agency are all over forty and the majority over fifty. A few years ago I surveyed every national board or commission or committee of a very large Protestant body. Out of the hundreds of persons who were members of these policy- and priority-setting agencies only four were reported to be in the twenty-four to thirty-four age range. And, believe it or not, all four of them were on the Board of Pensions. There was not one young person on any agency between seventeen and twenty-four representing any group except the college student organization—no military men, no young workers, no vocational students, no young professionals. One can only conclude that we plan without the generation.

The young can help us solve our problem. But they will also bring changes which in all likelihood we would rather not face. To date, we have chosen to go without them rather than have to listen to their demands and their reforms. The critical questions are, where is it getting us? How long will we continue?

five

*Revolution in Piety*_____

Piety is a word which is greatly worked and greatly mis-understood and misused by Americans, both Christians and non-Christians. To try to deal with it requires that we restate the basic meaning of the word. Piety means the manner in which one exercises his obedience, loyalty, or devotion to that in which he puts trust or belief. To put it in other words, piety is the form of expression of what one believes.

But, since we are here concerned with piety as it relates to us as Christians, *piety is the manner in which one exercises his obedience, loyalty, and devotion to Jesus Christ and to God.*

SETTING THINGS STRAIGHT

In order to conduct a useful exploration into the revolution which is occurring with regard to piety, it is essential to try to examine the manner in which most Americans are accustomed to using this word or its derivatives. In general, piety, pietism, pious, and pietistic are all used as if they described only a collection of disliked religious attitudes and habits (disciplines).

First, and foremost, *piety is the practice of devotion and obedience.* That means that everyone who has an order of values and beliefs by which he responds to his daily experiences is in the very response exercising his piety.

The exercise of piety is like the inhabitants of a remote mountain valley whose only entrance road was blocked by a huge rock that rolled down the hill. It fell in a precarious position, and to go near it was very dangerous. The people of the oldest village in the valley looked upon the rock as just one more sign of an evil god, and they were afraid of it, so they carved a new path around the mountain. The people of the middle village looked upon the rock as being very dangerous and walked very cautiously around it because they thought God would at any moment let the rock fall down and crush those with whom he was displeased. The people of the holy village sought to control the rock through prayer, gathering daily for intercessions concerning the rock, yet expressing their acceptance of God's will if the rock should fall. The people of new village, believing God to hold them responsible, explored the rock and, discovering a way it could be fastened to the hillside, employed the engineer to secure it and remove the danger.

In all these situations the people acted differently be-

91

cause each had a different set of value systems and religious beliefs. Yet in every instance their response was in and of itself an act of piety. It was their response to the problem according to what they believed. Their action was based on their own beliefs, and to the best of their ability they were obedient to what they believed. Our present conditioning will cause us to view some of these as being quite pietistic. For example, those who do nothing but pray . . . but piety is acting out what you believe.

So a second conclusion is: *wherever there is belief, there is also piety.* For everything which we believe influences our behavior and our responses. Piety is the visible form which we give to our internalized belief and value system. Piety is behavior, action, response. It can be identified, seen, felt, noticed, and known by others.

Third, what is viewed as an appropriate pietistic response under one set of beliefs would be inappropriate under another set of beliefs. *The forms of behavior serve to demonstrate the belief.* If one experiences what is perceived to be new truth but continues to practice the old form, his life is incongruent; his action is not in keeping with his belief. There have been times in human history when certain beliefs became established deeply and for generations. With a stabilized world view, the forms of expression gradually took on more authority than they actually had. For example, when man believed that the world was flat, sailors believed that somewhere out there was the *edge*. Then a wild idea began to circulate that the world was round! A sailor could now set sail to go around the world to the other side. He could now act differently because he believed differently. His belief system and value system had changed, and his visible expressions of them, his piety, also were changed. It now made sense to sail west to get east.

Piety changes as beliefs change. Now in a static world this fourth conclusion would have little meaning, since only a few new "truths" would be apt to be assimilated into the belief system at any one time. Wherever men began to accept new truths and act on them, they were often the object of ridicule, ostracism, or even severe punishment. One of the chief dispensers of such hostile and negative treatment was the church. Men were condemned to torture and death for holding some "new heresy" which was in fact not heresy at all but truth. The church was often the defender of the old pietistic forms long after a new truth and belief was clearly established. And defending the old form, it sought to use its long-accumulated power, might, authority, and influence to punish any whose piety revealed a new belief was alive in their minds.

NEW BELIEFS CALL FOR NEW PIETY

We are living in a time of both a passing piety and an emerging piety. We are seeing the disappearance of an old system of beliefs and the breaking forth of a new one, or perhaps new ones, both parallel and in rapid sequence.

Our times are often defined as an age of indecisiveness. When man does not know what he believes, or what to believe, he is without the core of belief and values on which he can act out his response to whatever may be occurring, even if it is to all appearances demanding some response of him. Even then only a great amount of fear will cause a man to behave in ways which conflict with his basic beliefs.

The necessity to make decisions accelerates the process of review and change that occurs in one's belief system. On the other hand, the habit of making a given response to a particular situation is sometimes difficult to bring under examination, even when one is reminded that new truths are calling both the old belief and its pietistic response into question. But all these conglomerate alternatives, transitions, and resistances are very much a reality for everyone who is alive today. The changing nature of life is almost beyond comprehension as fact. The crisis of piety comes when one attempts to integrate the changes into a system of belief and from that arrive at appropriate response forms, i.e., piety, which express one's loyalty and devotion to these new truths.

What are some of the elements of this change, and how do they strike us?

THE PASSING PIETY

The passing piety can be understood by the basic assumptions and principles of its posture. The beliefs behind the practices are most important. "Christians are saved! Others are unsaved!"

Christians were set apart from the rest of the human race. That was a virtue which was deliberately taught and practiced. To be saved meant that one had confessed, professed, and been baptized as a believing Christian. To be saved moved one from the ranks of the unsaved world into the camp of God. It was impossible to keep perspective with such terms and attitudes, so that soon the whole world was not just saved or unsaved; it had become likewise good or evil, white or black, and there was no middle ground. "Either you are for me or you are against me." No place in between existed. With this was to be linked another concept which would set the whole world not only in different camps but in tension.

"Christians Are Fishers of Men." The unsaved (meaning without Christian baptism) people were the concern of God. And the saved were to cast their nets (and hooks) amongst the others and "catch" them (by hook or by net!). So that's what happened. We cast nets in the American wilderness, in the new industrial slums, and with a mighty heave landed some hooks and nets as far away as Africa, Asia, and South America. And in they came! There were nets down on all sides, and wherever the fish were to be found, the fishermen got a catch. The unsaved were landed by fear, as if one started at one end of a slough and walked full abreast to the other end, scaring the carp into the nets already provided there to free those fish from such a muddy place. And many were landed by talking them in, just as a control tower operator might talk down a pilot to the runway on which he wanted him.

The catch was good. The success of the Christians confirmed the feeling that saving others was their main business. And so we entered the era when crews of fishermen began to compete with other crews of fishermen.

Denominations Were "God's Wineskins." The denominations took hardened form and accented their differences, though these were minor matters. The consequence of this effort resulted in competitive recruiting procedures that still are exercised with some sophistication in every major new suburb in America. Fortunately this plan did not go well in every nation as it did in the United States. The hardening of the followers of this group, or some other, resulted in the formation of what social scientists today would call "closed systems." That is, each denomination became a church in and of itself. It sought to demonstrate that it was self-sufficient (of course with God's divine undergirding). So there were Methodists and Baptists and Presbyterians and Catholics and Campbellites (with musical instruments) and the Campbellites (without musical instruments).

The more the denominations accented their different and distinctive elements of doctrine and practice, the more they neglected the great body of Christian teaching as it applied to all mankind. The more they sought to "rescue the perishing" and proselyte one another's catch, the more their preaching was confined to the threat and the snare devices which played on men's emotions. The more the gospel was viewed as being the good guys saving the bad guys, the more Christian teaching was neglected or, with the thrust of the Sunday school movement, aimed at the children and youth.

Taught to Be Church Members (Rise of Privatism). The new denominations now had strength, membership, a bit of history behind them, and with this came the inevitable expectation for loyalty and devotion. To be a good church member meant attending services every time they were held, giving your tithe to the church (or the preacher, as the case may have been), praying regularly for the church to be "upheld," and soon would come the explosion of church organization which would require that one take and fulfill various church offices. Suddenly a Christian was measured by the way he worked *in* the church! And the world had two spheres—one the company of the church (all saints, if you please) and the other the world out there filled with those still unsaved, and all those who belonged to other denominations. So Christians had now withdrawn from the evils of the world in order to be faithful to the church.

The result was widespread idolatry which continues. The church organization and activities were substituted as the ultimate work and practice of Christians. Members became churchmen first and perhaps Christians second. The church became a seductive idol that rapidly eroded the energy and influence of Christians. The Christians ceased to love God and took to loving the church. The church ceased to preach God's will and judgment and took to adoring and adorning itself. It ceased to feed the hungry and bought stocks. It ceased to follow Jesus and began to follow Dale Carnegie and Norman Peale. The church became a ghetto, cut off from the passing events, isolated and privatistic, believing that it could survive in such a state. Then began the decay and rot of its moral fiber.

The church vows said, "I will be loyal to the (you name it) church and uphold it with my prayers, my presence, my gifts, and my service," or other words and phrases to that effect. A church which was created in tension with the world outside that church must have ways of sustaining its distinctiveness and clearly keeping itself apart from that *world* (which no one any longer recalled that God had once loved). So there emerged a strong effort to standardize Christian piety (generally in denominational forms). They *would do* some things—hold church offices, go to church, read the Bible, attend prayer meeting, teach

Sunday school, have grace at meals, seek to save the un-saved, serve lunch to the Rotarians' and preachers' meetings, pray for and support their church—and they would be clear that they *would not do* other things—drink wine, beer, or liquor, attend movies, play cards, go to Sunday ball games, associate with sinners, use tobacco, say four-letter words aloud, belong to any secret groups (except the Masonic Lodge, the Order of the Eastern Star, and other such unquestionably virtuous groups). All these dos and don'ts became the piety of the church and strangely, though they sought to be distinctive, this pattern was almost uniform among the Protestant groups.

What we see today in the transition of piety is the demise of this rather brittle system of forms by which faith was to be expressed. Many of these pietistic forms are almost completely gone, but in spite of that one finds that it is almost an act of indecency to advocate openly setting them aside. There is no doubt but that such advocacy can lead to ostracism by the church. As the renewal movement makes steady gains in the church, the conservative elements will take stronger and more rigid stands on the things they hold important. This will soon lead to compulsive legalism, as they become more desperate to hold onto the past. Some, hopefully only a few, will be ready to launch a twentieth-century purge with all the ingredients of what might be called an "enlightened" Inquisition.

THE EMERGING PIETY

If the passing piety saw an emphasis on the differences and the minor aspects of Christian life and mission, then the emerging piety surely accents the major themes and elements of the Christian message.

Honest to God. There is more in these three words than a book title. The desire for honesty is probably the underlying strength of the emerging piety. The transition is from *niceness* as the ultimate of Christian virtue to a posture of realistic honesty, regardless of its consequences. Niceness is no longer considered a Christian virtue without honesty. Rather, honesty is the prerequisite to the emerging piety.

This readiness for honesty draws quick blood. The church is not a healthy institution. The state of the church is quite imperfect; it is far less than the kingdom of God come on earth. The church which has been reported as having such success must face the fact that by its own statistical reports it is not only failing to grow at a rate comparable with the national population increase, it is even losing membership during this time of population explosion. The emerging piety quickly recognizes that old success notices mean very little now, if ever. The new pietists are willing to love the church *with* her imperfections, so long as the church does not try to claim their first loyalty—a commitment which belongs to God in Jesus. They can honestly face faults, falterings, and failures. They even value the frank recognition of such, claiming that, if these are in our history, we can only learn by acknowledging them. Those exercising the new piety are quick to separate what "is" from sentimentality, naïveté, blind optimism. If plans and proposals are unrealistic, then let them be known for what they are. If membership rolls are "padded," correct them to reflect the true membership. If there is bad news about, face it,

99

hear it, and, if it needs to be known by others, see to it. When there is good news about, treat it the same.

Criteria of Effectiveness. If the hard facts of statistical losses were not enough, the "report" process of the churches also indicates that there is a widespread and still spreading dissatisfaction with uniform planning and programming either by national bureaucracies of the denominations or by regional or state level structures. The measure of success, since the leveling off of the growth period, has been shifted to the kinds of internal success congregations and groups of congregations have experienced in "bringing off," sometimes "putting over," the national emphases, conference or synod or diocesan programs, or other simultaneous efforts of one kind or another, ranging from fund collections for sundry causes to membership drives to individual reading programs. Local clergy and laity are making it quite clear that they are not satisfied that their purpose is to be the program promoters and organizers of one big push after another. While at the time of this writing there are still some efforts of this nature being attempted, they have already been sharply cut back. The message from the "grass roots" is getting through to the program-planning agencies of the various denominations. It is my own observation that much of the program emphases that now seem to be an undesired "burden" to local leadership is actually set at synod, presbytery, conference, or diocesan level. If this hunch is accurate, it means that the local representatives are still voting in the programs that they feel reluctant to continue to implement. In either event, it is clear that it is only a matter of time until local congregations and other groups will assert their concern and refuse to promote programs which do not have a kind of indigenous rationale.

Into this freedom from canned and handed-down programs has come a new, vigorous, and creative struggle with the question, if success is not measured by all these statistics and all these programmatic efforts, then what shall we do? Another and more precise way to ask the question is: what is any particular group of Christians being called to do? What must be done through the life of a given group of Christians in order that they may at least have sought to have been obedient? By what criteria can we measure effectiveness?

This search for more useful criteria for effectiveness goes on. It has become clear that to pursue new criteria forces one into serious *theological study and restudy of the biblical sources of the church itself.* Others are also finding some encouragement in their search as they recognize the necessity to *know the world about them.* Calling upon sociologists, planners, futurists, developers, political and governmental leaders, they are discovering that to seek God's will for us in any given place may require that we have a complete and comprehensive perspective of the trends and problems of that area. Others are finding that they must *identify with the deprived and dependent peoples* of a city or region if they are to know what God's will is for those who are in so obvious need of such basic elements of the good life as food, housing, dignity, and civil rights.

A few who have pioneered longer and have attempted to implement new ministries within the framework of new statements or understandings of mission have encountered the next difficult task—the renewal of the congregation(s).

How can members who have made peace with Zion be brought out of these present attitudes and led to live with a fearless obedience to a God still transforming the world? The equipping of the church, as it now is, for ministry of a radically different nature is no small necessity. It is a task which now besets every faculty in every seminary, all national church agencies, and local leadership with equal urgency and difficulty. Simply put, the problem is that both the laity and the clergy joined the church and assumed their roles in a different era. Then came the multifaced revolution of the sixties, making it essential to seek a renewal of church in this last third of the twentieth century. In this new task the old roles are being redefined—whether one likes it or not.

In the Public Arena. While our saving missions of days past often were located on the street corners of the slums and skid rows of our congested cities, they were there to save and snare persons (souls) out of that and into the church. Today the oft-quoted verse of the sidewalk preacher, John 3:16, is now the foundation of a radically different kind of mission to the world. With eyes opened a bit more than before, we know now that all men have to live *in* the world. There is no escape from the world except death, and fewer people are sure just where that leads. So the declaration that "God loves the world" comes as a bold reminder for those who have condemned the world and tried desperately, if unsuccessfully, to live apart from it. Today the church is cautiously and reluctantly beginning to move into the public arena for the sake of the whole society. The poor, the minorities, the outcast, the powerless, the illiterate, the deviant and variant peoples have come much more clearly on the agenda of the renewal church today. Our response is not so much words of assurance nor promises of the next life as it is a movement to be a champion of those for whom no champion has been forthcoming. To champion the people who have been without voice (to say nothing of the greater and more basic essentials of existence) in today's modern metropolis is to come out of the cloistered walls of the church and walk into the public arena. And this is where the emerging piety is taking us. And with it public speaking becomes more important than pulpiteering, community organizing a greater priority than church groups for men and women. Risking becomes a necessity, not an option.

The Ecumenical Movement. The tide toward ecumenicity is one of the clearest signs of an emerging piety. Perhaps it is worth pointing out that with this emerging form of piety it is already possible to foresee the demise of the great denominationalism which segmented the larger church and often even pitted one section against another with bitter relationships. The ecumenical movement carries its participants in a direction which has, in many ways, already reversed the trend of the segmentation and division of the church in the first half of the twentieth century.

However, all is not glitter in this development. There exist two routes for the church in the ecumenical thrust. Albert van den Heuvel of Geneva has termed the two routes as "churchly ecumenism" or "worldly ecumenism." I make no apology in clearly believing that the direction of churchly ecumenism is nothing more than the drive for Christian unity. Unity is a worthy and important goal to be sought because of the brokenness of the church in the world today. Ecumenism, however, that stops at a unified Christian church will at once begin to falter, for it will have not found its mission. Church unity is not the Christian mission.

Only a concept of worldly ecumenism can open to us an adequate perspective for identifying and defining our mission in the world taking shape now. Ecumenism is by definition an inclusive concept, meaning "the whole inhabited earth." Any view which the church has of itself short of its participation in the affairs of the whole inhabited earth will immediately limit and restrict her ability to be with and for all men everywhere. This view of worldly ecumenism does not require that the church merge with the state, nor does it require that the Christian peoples be uniformly organized. Rather, it requires that the Christian church exercise a concern for all men everywhere, regardless of their race, color, creed, nationality, status, sex, age, generation, and even planetary origin. It requires that the church be aware of and prepared to respond to the whole sphere of human experience from personal and developmental needs to the public functions of citizen, neighbor, contributor, volunteer, worker, student, and so forth.

It is this inclusive posture which is essential. And to carry the present church to an awareness of this definition of the scope and arena of our Christian mission will require considerable effort as well as time. It is this underlying attitude and spirit about the whole world that sets meaning to any concept of the kingdom of God.

Realistic and Relative. In the emerging piety a high value is placed on realism. It may be an overcompensation. The

104

church has been perceived as naïve, starry-eyed, or just plain unrealistic. For whatever reason, realism has been stressed in recent years. It is this emphasis on realism that has helped to bring about the frank recognition of what once was called success as less than God's will for the church in our day. It is this realism that has enabled small, disciplined groups of young clergy and laity to expect of one another a kind of awareness and a level of being informed which was seldom present a decade earlier. It is this realism, perhaps inherited in part from the contribution of the scientific method of learning and problem solving in public schools, that has caused leaders in many sectors of life to express encouragement for those who are seeking to live a new piety as they seek a renewed church.

Relativism has been the subject of most every significant book in the field of ethics in recent years. Simply put, the idea is that blacks aren't all the same shade of black, and whites aren't all the same shade of white, and what's in the middle isn't all the same shade of gray. Realism goes hand in glove with relativism, for together they implement an evolutionary process.

The emerging piety also brings a new awareness and utilization of power into the thinking of Christians.

In defiance of the cliché, "Religion and politics do not mix," some urban churches have recognized that the basic decisions about the life of people in the city are made in the pyramids of power, especially those of business and politics. . . .

Church members in these churches are being urged to participate in the political life of their city as a part of their ministry in Christ's name.[1]

105

In the sixties the church has learned much about community organization from leaders in the field such as Saul Alinsky. Community organization represents the operational arm of the new concept of power. Now we are seeing significant efforts to help powerless people organize themselves in order to set goals for themselves, their neighbors and neighborhoods.

This new use of power as a tool for ministry is plied within the two concepts discussed here, namely, relativism and realism. With power from being organized and having clearly defined and feasible goals, the church is now able to join with others to assist in *their* efforts to find a place for themselves in our society. The recognition of power as a tool allows the church to share in the initiative needed to combat evil wherever it exists. The new piety has as one of its elements an aggressiveness seldom present in our preceding history.

The End of Negativism. I feel about this new emerging piety among Christians as does David Wilson of Nashville, who expressed himself recently. When his city had voted into law a proposition allowing liquor to be sold by the ounce in the city, he commented with words to the effect that the significance of the vote was not that liquor could now be bought by the ounce (legally), but that he believed that the vote was the first indication that "the city had broken the back of negativism" which had so long dominated thinking on issues far more crucial and important than the proposition which was then being raised.

I find that young churchmen and young people outside and away from the church show some interest in the church if they discover it in the form of the new emerging piety.

At least, it seems relevant to the times in which they are living. It may not appeal to them as a style of life they choose to believe in and exercise, but it does command a kind of respect which is seldom present when they are facing the form of piety which is now beginning to pass.

six

*If the Medium Is the Message!*_____

Marshall McLuhan's recent writing has lifted up the impact that media themselves convey a message regardless of the "content" that may also be dispatched via them. He has suggested that

all media work us over completely. They are so pervasive in their personal, political, economic, aesthetic, psychological, moral, ethical, and social consequences that they leave no part of us untouched, unaffected, unaltered. The medium is the massage. Any understanding of social and cultural change is impossible without a knowledge of the way media work as environments. All media are extensions of some human faculty.[1]

McLuhan defines his meaning further in *Understanding Media.*

For the "message" of any medium or technology is the change of scale or pace or pattern that it introduces into human affairs. . . .

This fact merely underlies the point that "the medium is the message" because it is the medium that shapes and controls the scale and form of human association and action. The content or uses of such media are as diverse as they are ineffectual in shaping the form of human association. Indeed, it is only too typical that the "content" of any medium blinds us to the character of the medium.[2]

McLuhan's work implies that (1) if new forms are needed, then old forms have to be evaluated as to the degree of their relevance. For whom are they meaningful? How long will they be meaningful? What reason is there for continuing them, when we know that people are formed by their continued use? (2) Where old forms are found to be ineffectual, they must be discarded *now*. The idea that old forms should be kept around while we look for new forms should be abandoned. It is important to stop the medium which provides a hollow and negative experience as soon as it is known to do so. To hang onto an inadequate form for the sake of having a form is idolatry or just plain foolishness. If it is possible that all earth and its forms of life and the resulting civilization came forth from void and chaos, then I suggest that the allowing for a climate of chaos and absence of forms may in itself be a medium which carries the urgent message of that moment—namely, that we are without adequate forms and are in search of those which will have meaning. That may make us relevant again. My friend Noble Groves of Oklahoma was right when he used to say that in the church we have a great capacity to turn on all kinds of new faucets, but we never turn any old ones off. It is an accurate illustration of our fear to risk closing down something that is already running —even if its worth has receded to an occasional drip! (3) Forms for the celebration of life (in our case "in Christ") are born through living. They are not products from the scientific laboratory. They are not born in think tanks, though the ability to think and interact with people who hold differing perspectives will be essential. They are not born in ivory towers or pulpits or sanctuaries or weekly one-hour meetings of worship committees. They are *found*— not born. They are the common reality which we know to be true and which we have experienced in our daily lives to the extent that we can reflect on the meaning that was *there* and recall it through establishing some form which incorporates its general meaning through one experience or a series of experiences. Celebration occurs *after the fact* but with an awareness that *the fact has meaning now* and will carry us safely into the future.

The bulk of our effort to form new ways of celebrating life has been focused on the events, the acts, the facts, and the trends of our times. McLuhan suggests that the processes by which all this change is occurring are the root of our life experience. For example, the church tries to identify with the different segments of the contemporary population. We have explored the necessity of having special ministries for the young generation, for campus students, for the military establishment, for Negroes in both urban and rural areas. The poor are segmented, and the rich are segmented. There are churches for Indians and churches

110

for Spanish Americans. But what is the process in our society which has resulted in causing us to become so sensitive to our differences? Why have we found ourselves coming to the same situation with one minority group after another? Suppose the bigger process at work is the development and establishment of *pluralism* as an accepted ingredient in our society. If that defines the larger trend or process occurring, then we can see that, though it is happening throughout our nation, it is influenced by forces both within and outside our culture. There is an international or world move toward acceptance, equality, and pluralism.

So our question becomes, what is the Christian experience in a pluralistic world in which we discover the meanings of life? And how do we celebrate those meanings? What is so good about life, as a Christian life, in a pluralistic society that it is "good news"? The good news of the process is that the world has become a society, especially with regard to mutual respect and dignity. If that is so, then we must celebrate that event in our time. If the process of pluralism creates the danger of dividing people and causing conflict and war, then Christians must seek those dimensions of life that are good news to a mankind caught in this predicament. It will have to be sought through experience. Those experiencing will find a perspective which brings forth forms to celebrate the meaning of unity in a pluralistic culture rather than segmentation and disunity. If the media of our electronic age require the full spectrum of our senses, then celebration will no doubt be of a similar nature.

COMMUNICATION EXPERIENCE
OF THE NEW GENERATION

We are being challenged today by the generation which
has reached adolescence and now early adulthood. The
world of electronic circuitry has been the only world they
have ever known.

The television generation is a grim bunch. It is much more
serious than children of any other period—when they were
frivolous, more whimsical. The television child is more earnest,
more dedicated.

Most often the few seconds sandwiched between the hours of
viewing—the "commercials"—reflect a truer understanding of
the medium. There simply is no time for the narrative form,
borrowed from earlier print technology. The story line must
be abandoned. Up until very recently, television commercials
were regarded as simply a bastard form, or vulgar folk art. They
are influencing contemporary literature.[3]

The contemporary young man or woman lives in a mythical world of electronically processed data which he receives
immediately and in clear and direct detail. This produces
a generation which perceives and understands in different
and more inclusive ways than we who are older. We continue to rely on the old tools to do our jobs for us, or, if
we do take up some of the new tools, we expect them to do
the old work in old ways. We find ourselves able to comprehend the element of time but not space and multisensual
effects. We can see how something always done might be
done faster. However, it seems impossible to set out radically to unlearn our old ways in order to relearn new ways.
Our goals themselves are no longer appropriate, to say
nothing of the methods. "The young today reject goals.

They want roles—R-O-L-E-S. That is, total involvement. They do not want fragmented, specialized goals or jobs." [4] We want to tinker! We want to use the new media to accomplish our old goals. But, if the medium is the message, then our offices, our classrooms, our training centers, our sanctuaries, our pulpits, and our forms of entertainment all become the local "theater of the absurd" from the viewpoint of the young.

The youth of today are not permitted to approach the traditional heritage of mankind through the door of technological awareness. This only possible door for them is slammed in their faces by a rear-view-mirror society.

The young today live mythically and in depth. But they encounter instruction in situations organized by means of classified information—subjects are unrelated, they are visually conceived in terms of a blueprint. Many of our institutions suppress all the natural direct experience of youth, who respond with untaught delight to the poetry and the beauty of the new technological environment, the environment of popular culture. It could be their door to all past achievement if studied as an active (and not necessarily benign) force.

The student finds no means of involvement for himself and cannot discover how the educational scheme relates to his mythic world. [5]

Ross Snyder tells a story which may serve to illustrate this mythical world–real world dimension. In a speech to a group of architects, he recounted the experience of the people of a German city experiencing a terrible flood. Naturally, what the TV reports is "real world." But these persons were so conditioned to recognize the real world of the television screen and to rely on it for accurate information that some of them had to be taken bodily from their own flooding homes because of their interest in the TV reports of the flood. This illustrates both the strong identification with the screen of the TV as a reality-providing vehicle and also the irony of becoming so completely caught up in one dimension of reality that another dimension of the same reality becomes irrelevant. The viewers knew, from TV reports, that their section of the city was being flooded, but somehow that information was not as influential on them as the desire to continue to receive data about the flood.

Another story is told of a man who sat in a neighbor's home watching TV with compulsive interest while his own home was being shown afire.

What does all this mean? It means that television can have a greater total impact on people than the experience of day-to-day life. Why? For one reason, the TV can eliminate time and distance and status from the barriers that sometimes make it impossible for us to be a part of something. The TV makes us a part of places where we cannot be present. It actually enlarges our potential for receptivity to the point that we are a part of the whole world and outer space as well. And that is access which no one in all history had before television.

So the new generation expects involvement on the scene whether we are undertaking a look at the future, the depths of the ocean, a battle on another continent, the presidential mansion, the moon, or a riot. He is capable of perceiving with several senses simultaneously, and communication that is not of that sort somehow seems to be marginal, unimportant communication. Look at the way the church is currently attempting to communicate with this new generation!

WHAT MESSAGE ARE WE SENDING?

To gain any assistance from this new awareness of the nature of communication, we must examine the various elements of our own life and practices on which messages are being carried. To see some of the immediately obvious implications, notice two specifics of our contemporary church practice and the kind of messages which well may be carried via the media themselves. (Again, this is not an attempt to evaluate the topical content of such experiences, only the message the medium itself carries.)

The message via the church young adult groups. The average young adult group in a church represents an escape from good theological concepts of the church and its laity. It also has become a means by which the people who control the church escape confrontation with younger ideas and idealism. It brings to the church the undemocratic white southern mentality of "separate but equal"-ism —which is indeed separate and never equal. By the continuation of these groups in such a status we are systematically bringing the church to decadence.

Let's reconstruct a typical group and use it to examine the meanings conveyed by its existence. The Pairs and Spares class is a young adult group with an age range from twenty to thirty-seven. Some of its members are single (Spares), though most are married (Pairs). The class is a part of the church's educational work. The chief advisor is the director of religious education. There are elected officers and chairmen for recreation and devotions. These

115

plan special events or line up teachers. The main meeting is Sunday morning. This usually consists of:

1. coffee and doughnuts; fifteen minutes but may take up to thirty minutes. A chance to meet newcomers, see old friends, and make friendships with those in the group who most appeal to one.

2. the devotional; three to five minutes. Typically a hymn, a prayer, the Bible lesson, a poem, a devotional thought, another hymn and prayer.

3. announcements and introduction of the teacher.

4. the *lesson;* on rare occasions taught by a class member but more likely an older person. The "lesson" is usually approved material from the denominational publisher. A lecture-type presentation summarizing the material and some discussion questions follow.

5. an offering.

6. a head-count report to the Sunday school officials.

There are many groups for which this model is not representative, but it is representative of the majority of church young adult groups.

What does an experience of this nature carry as its message (massage)? First, theologically these persons are the laity, full members of the church of Christ and generally members of the denomination as well. In this role they are expected to assume full responsibility in and for the life of the church, and particularly as it exists in the local congregation to which they are related.

But in fact and practice the young adult group often provides an alternative to full membership. The young adults have their children in church school and keep some tie to the church. They can avoid the demands of time and money expected of full members. The older members are happy to see the young adults around the church and glad they are not pressing for places of leadership, authority, decision making, or bringing their young ideas to major meetings. So the young adult group exists! The message is that it is a "holding operation," a halfway stop, and not really *in* the church. Those who want to exert leadership serve the young adult group. Since they look toward the day when they might "make it" into the real church structure, they are willing to provide whatever level of cooperation is requested of them. They are apt to be more loyal to the church fathers than to the young adult group, at which time the group becomes a pawn in the hands of unseen authorities. The decisions about what it may do and may not do are handed down. The freedom it has is limited from above without consultation. The rights it may exert are restricted from above and without reprieve. The group acclimates itself to a holding operation.

I am reminded of a description of one young adult who was asked to complete the open-ended sentence, "Being a Christian today is like. . . ." He wrote, "Being all dressed up for a party two hours early and being put out in the backyard and told not to get dirty and to come when called." That is the message of the medium in many instances. By its existence the church and the young adult can avoid the confrontation they should have. They are mutually satisfied with an escape structure to avoid the reality of each other.

When it comes to the life of the larger church, these young adult groups have little or no authority. They are not consulted about the ethical decisions which the church faces. They do not have a say about the policies and practices which are appropriate for the church to set. They have no way to recommend the use of money which the church receives. They have no influence on the priorities the board of officials will determine. Generally, they just aren't a part of what happens. They may be busy churchmen, but they aren't effective Christians. They generally have little interest beyond their own group activities and members.

Most young adults visit a few times and don't come back. Others may attend regularly for some time and suddenly disappear. What such groups finally communicate is that young adults aren't really needed in any vital sense. This communication from the medium itself is constantly making its impact on all concerned. It results in young adults having been thoroughly taught that church membership is a marginal relationship for the young. The young churchman is to wait, delay, put off acting as a fully responsible member of the congregation. No wonder these groups build up effective defenses against the church influencing what they do. These groups become privatistic, withdrawn, and either reject or become sharply estranged from and indifferent to the Christian mission in the twentieth century.

A second message which comes from participation in these groups is that getting acquainted with other persons is important. This desire for friendships is what Erik Erikson calls the need for intimacy. It operates in the individual as an urge to acquire intimate friendships and relationships. Intimacy can be related to experiences of belonging, being "in," having memberships, being included, loved, needed, and wanted. Isolation, the opposite of intimacy, is related to experiences of loneliness, separateness, being left out, excluded, passed by, the wallflower.

In these young adult groups some persons will find close friends. Ross Snyder suggests that everyone must belong to a small society of as many as five or more persons—a societal relationship which has primary meaning to each of its members, a group to which persons are loyal. Persons who do not have this kind of relationship with others are lonely and isolated. For these purposes, the cliques, once frowned on as being exclusive, are now seen as essential to the welfare of individuals. Any large group or class is healthiest if it has several such subgroups. Smaller clusters of people who appreciate one another are not necessarily a destructive device ruining the larger membership.

However, church young adult groups frequently view themselves as "a study group." They contend that study efforts should take precedence over the socializing function. Some groups constantly suppress the need for friendships and emphasize only the learning dimension. They end up establishing a negative judgment on friends and fun, making friendships, fellowship, and socializing a kind of illegitimate dimension of the group experience. They neglect a basic human need of persons.

Some young adult groups communicate that life is fun, people are interdependent, and friendships are important. They believe the existence of the group can provide possibilities for such friendships. May their tribe increase!

Third, the learning dimension of these groups is another clear message. Frankly, it says again and again that study and learning are not taken seriously at the church. There is

119

little chance to determine what will be studied, to say nothing of questions such as how and where it might be studied. The "teaching" process is generally given precedence over the learning process. The material is almost always planned in sequence and always on the principle of connections. Little leeway is left for individual struggling with some of the variables. The prevailing attitude toward a "lesson" is that the Bible or the church does have *the* answer to a given situation, and the goal is to get it said clearly so everyone "sees" it. The use of resources is shoddy, unintellectual, and implies the crutch method. The awareness that individuals set their own learning pace is not honored. The urgency of making judgments about those things which seem "controversial" never takes precedence over just studying about them. And certainly one would be considered a starry-eyed lunatic if he genuinely expected that the study life in such groups would actually make significant and noticeable changes in the life style and life ways of the members of the group. Teaching and learning are sloppy, and no one expects them to be otherwise.

The fourth message implies that devotionals are a form of worship. That's absurd. Most of the devotionals are sentimentalized and virtually useless. The *Upper Room* mentality that prevails is that the group must have a devotion every day, in as much the same place as possible and following the same procedure regularly. It is mechanized meditation which does not require the presence of the Creator or the inventor. It can run automatically and "never hurt anyone." The systematized approach prevails over the kind of world and life experience represented in the members of the group.

These devotionals are about the worst possible experience that could be made available to a new generation of media-minded people. They destroy any desire to pursue the meaningfulness of a worship experience in other avenues. Too often they resemble the regular service of worship or vice versa.

Fifth, the young adult group does teach something about attendance and quantity. The primary criterion for evaluating a meeting is the number who attended. The success of a given meeting is apt to be measured by one or more of these measures—the goal for that day, the all-time attendance record, the attendance last week, or the percentage of total membership. And, if the digital total doesn't add up to the president's expectations or the director's goal, then there is probably a little reprimand or a pep rally. The attitude toward numbers and digits teaches again and again that they are our ultimate concerns, the real goals of the class leadership, the leadership of the Sunday school and the church, too.

Sixth, one can also get a good training in spectatorship from these groups. Most of the members seldom do any active leading or even participation. They attend, pay, are counted, applaud (or say, "That was very interesting"), then depart with a note in their mind of the time and place for the next game . . . er, ah, meeting.

Finally, another learning that is reinforced is that a cup of coffee sure helps on a Sunday morning.

The message via the sermon. The sermon is one of the most common approaches which the church uses to communicate with its own constituency and with others. It is probably second to buildings. For it seems that, though many have tried for long years, little real progress has been made in replacing the assumption that going to church means going to hear a sermon. In the thinking of many, many people, *it* is central. This is true even with people who regularly participate and worship in congregations where the worship is, at least in my judgment, liturgy centered. They view the sermon as the main event, no matter where it is located or how long or short it may be.

Stephen Rose has suggested that, if a minister can't preach well, he shouldn't preach. I agree. And, if his suggestion is taken seriously, a great many of my friends will begin to examine alternatives to preaching. The seminaries seem to be devoted to the sermon form of communication. Instead of assuming all are to be preachers, men should come from seminary with alternative forms for communicating God's good news to men today. The knowledge of the twentieth century judges the sermonic form as a weak communicating tool. But both clergy and laity cling to it as if it had some extraordinary potential. We love the form more than we want to communicate the "good news." Could it be we have little to say? I know only a few dozen persons who should attempt to preach via sermons more than once a month. To get a perspective on his preaching, a pastor might ask some of us church bureaucrats. We are the sympathetic, empathetic, and frequently the most discerning hearers. We want the "good news" to come through in every communication attempt. But the pew filler hears too many words and too little message of good news.

Five basic realities regarding the sermon should be examined. They are not new. The irony (or tragedy) is that we seldom see "preachers" doing anything about them.

1. One-way communication: That is the medium of sermons. They are designed to talk to people. They stem from a premise that he who is doing the sermonizing has something of such importance and such clarity that it can be accomplished in the limitations of one-way communication. There is no way to get a give-and-take going *on the spot.* In order to inquire about or contest any aspect of the sermon, one must stay afterward, corner the preacher, and hope to get a bit of give-and-take going. We live in a day when one-way communication has long been regarded as a sure way to confusion, distortion, misunderstanding, and, as often as not, a tuned-out audience of what at a casual glance appears to be hearers.

In a few isolated cases sermons are taking on the form of a dialogue. In even fewer situations the ground rule is that questions should come at any time. In a few more situations there are arrangements made in advance to discuss the sermon following the dismissal, often hours or even days later. In rare instances arrangements are made for members to be in on the homiletical preparation, hear the sermon, and critique it in light of their earlier work. By and large, it is a one-way communication attempt—an obsolete, at best limited tool for modern man. This is an age when dialogue is so clearly an urgent need that it has become a household word. Though it is late, it is not too late to shift to a better tool.

2. Abstract: About! The sermon as a vehicle relies on a procedure which tries to take the linear written word and talk about it. It is always in the *about* posture, seldom the *is-now* situation. The material often deals with abstractions, theological theories and concepts which are not only in-

tangible to begin with but often gain elusiveness as they fly by. In a day when man is accustomed to living with the real world wrapping around him from the television screen and the past and the future presenting themselves in tangible form in the den or living room, talking about abstractions is not a very sophisticated form of communication. Evidence is mounting that it has little worth. The church is so much out of the action that it can only speak *about* the *now* history of man.

3. Generalized information and interpretation: The sermon is a contrast to our contemporary data-oriented society. People want facts and significant, persuasive evidence. They no longer assume that "if the preacher says it's so, it's so." That day is gone, even in theological and religious matters. People are learned, informed, and educated. They insist that any leader know what he is talking about, and his pitch must "make sense" to them. The young generation is still asking the question of the young man in the Bible, "What must I do to be saved?" The language has changed, but the question is still asked. Today it sounds like this: "How can I make sense out of my life?" And that question comes frequently and from all quarters of the generation —those in church and those who have left the church. They have psychological data about themselves, sociological data on the world, cultural data on the society. They are now facing most of life's problems as adults. Today's world is complex. No wonder they want to make sense of it. One can destroy his life by a series of poor decisions. One can lose his way in all the confusion of people, data, problems, and offers of help. To be saved today is to find a way to make sense out of life.

But generalized platitudes, even with the trademark of the church or the Bible, will not be accepted as assumptions. Much of this generation has a low tolerance for being sheep. If we ever find them in the church, it will be as disciples. That will require all the skills and know-how of top-flight leadership, not just the steadiness and good intentions of a flockmaster.

4. From mouth to ear: Here we live in a day when "multimedia" is not just an idea. It is a practice. We experience media systems of several kinds sending their messages to us through a combination of our senses. But the sermon still relies almost solely on the mouth for transmitting and on the ear for reception. Educational research has indicated that this is the least effective of any possible communication system (except mute sign language where no common symbols are predetermined).

5. Standardized and linear: Finally, the sermon relies on the technique of the Gutenberg era. It is connected. It attempts to tie up every loose end, so that all is connected together. It tries to draw the learning or conclusion for the hearer. There is nothing for the hearer to do in the process. He is closed out. He cannot talk back. There is no built-in interval for which he must supply data or opinion; there is no hard data which may be assessed. In fact, he is hardly needed in order for it to have accomplished its effectiveness. We often hear the phrase that someone "delivered" a sermon. My newspaper man can deliver the paper whether I'm at home or out to lunch.

So the sermon must try to live as something significant with all this going against the medium itself. If that medium is supposed to represent what we believe, then I hope to see some changes in the sermonic efforts of those who read this. It is late, but not too late.

Buildings, programs, music, newspapers, radio and TV usage, bulletins, and signs all share in creating an image through themselves as media of the church's communication. The two primary arenas of communication with young adults are the group and the sermon. If these media communicate anything like the kind of message and/or massage that I have sketched here, the church is not sending the message it intends to be sending, and some radical homework is imperative.

*The Key of Christian Mission*_____

I have found the church to contain many clergymen and laymen who are genuinely concerned about the gap between the church and the new generation. Their intentions are good. Their efforts are seriously undertaken. They sometimes discover significant breakthroughs. But more often they meet with further frustration. I have found that very few churches have done thorough planning aimed at a new, effective ministry among young adults. Most seem to assume that, if they just jazz up what they are currently doing, young adults will flock to them. Churches *must* develop plans for mission to the new generation who are:

    adjacent to colleges or universities

    near military installations

    near several trade, technical, or business schools

surrounded by low-cost apartments or boardinghouses
close to large medical complexes
downtown large churches
near ghetto areas of predominantly young people
close to new generation centers such as East Village in
   New York, Haight-Ashbury in San Francisco, Old
   Town in Chicago.

I have found that most churches in these situations are aware of the young adult population around them but have not been able to involve many of them in the life and activities of a church program.

THE QUESTION OF INTENTIONS

A very current question that is asked in almost every church circle is whether evangelism means the concern for the spiritual life and eternal life of individuals or whether it is the effort of the church to assure all men an abundant life now. Is the church concerned about the private life of men or their public life? Are we a people with a message to individuals or to society? Is our primary concern for man's future life or his present life?

This question of what we intend to be or do among the new generation people must be answered before we can hope to effect a satisfactory relationship with them.

Current theological study is challenging the church to take its responsibility for the contemporary life of man with all seriousness. The exploration of space has brought an end to the concepts of heaven being out there and God being up there. Our scientific studies of life and space have exploded many of the myths on which Christians have built the case for another life. The impact of Freud and Frankl has left some clear information about the nature of the human spirit, the freedom of the individual, and the power of self-direction and self-determination. Erik Erikson has opened up the understanding of the developmental process in persons and the extent to which the various aspects of total development take on success or failure characteristics.

Recent studies of the character of church life and the way in which Christians have been giving themselves to the church have caused us to reexamine the theological basis for the church. With this study words like ministry, mission, renewal have sprung into our everyday conversations. The sociological and cultural trends which have been the subject of extensive study have suddenly pointed to the fact that the great issues affecting human life in this age have not been the issues to which the church has been giving itself.

Instead of withdrawing from the world, or denying that the world is the way it is, the church is rapidly moving to accept the task of living *in* the world, participating in its controversy, taking its share of responsibility for changing that which is inhumane, unethical, or destructive to men or societies. This is changing the nature of the church's work. It is not so much to build a great church as it is to further the possibility of a worthwhile society in which men may live abundantly. It is not escapism that is advocated, but involvement. Such involvement replaces so much talk about God and Jesus and the church with declarations about the rights, the place, and the dignity of every man. The involved church centers its mission on its own city, community, neighborhood, as clearly as it has in times past

129

sought to conduct missions in other nations or continents. It speaks less of loyalty to the institution and more about obligations to serve those who suffer indignities, inequalities, or who lack such basic essentials as food, work, housing, and health care.

Each congregation or cluster of congregations must make some clear decisions about their intentions in the midst of the new generation. If the intention is to get them to become members of the church, is that the sole intention or the long-range hope? Is the immediate intention to get them involved in activities or to involve ourselves in their activities? Do we want to save them from something? Or are we interested in giving a demonstration of the fact that we oppose those forces and events that make their lives difficult? Do we want to speak a word of correction to them, or do we have a word of affirmation? Or both? Every ministry with the new generation must self-consciously answer the question, what is it we hope will be the result of our efforts?

My answer to this question has been shaped by observing many attempts to communicate with the generation and the many responses of the generation. The church must be perceived as persons who do not know what it is like to be members of the new generation but are prepared to learn from them. We must be prepared to experience the hardships they know. We must make our best resources—minds, money, time—available for their support.

Efforts to do less than this, or to try some other beginning point, have always led to frustration and failure. George "Bill" Webber of the East Harlem Protestant Parish noted several years ago that "part of the frustration of much that the church does in our time may come from the fact that it is engaged in the wrong fight, giving its energy to battles that are finally irrelevant."

These who attempt this kind of ministry should be aware of a number of old assumptions about church work which are no longer true.

1. that ministry occurs only in and through local churches
2. that present patterns of evangelism and education and mission are too deeply established to change
3. that there is only one approach and it works for all situations
4. that what we are now doing is right; we just need to work at it harder
5. that the effectiveness of the church's work is really determined by its bishops, bureaucrats, clergy, rich laymen, and other authoritative persons
6. that some ideas are too extreme to try, even though there is reason to think they will be effective
7. that funds aren't available to support a good idea
8. that the answers to mission will be found through small study groups
9. that effectiveness in the future will still be measured on the old norms of success such as numbers and percentages
10. that present structures can be used for the basis of all new efforts, i.e., local churches, parishes, denominations, etc.
11. that new attempts can be kept to the side or back of the ongoing life and work of the church.

THE TIME TO TRY

It is now clear that we must undertake more new, bold efforts to identify with the new generation on their grounds. We must experiment with well-thought-out imaginative efforts that incorporate a message of genuine concern and self-giving. These messages must be communicated in things that are in the form of doing, not speaking. It is unlikely that more words, even if they are different ones, will prove to be adequate for the communication task that faces us. We must do those things which in their happening provide a clear statement of our intentions and our desire to be with the new generation.

Laity and clergy who believe that the church can be effective in the midst of the world must associate themselves and undertake these new ventures in Christian mission and ministry. Sometimes this can be done as a special project of a particular congregation or association. Or it may result in a strong opposing force in the congregation, saying, "We're the church. We're here, and they know where we are. We can't lower our standards and take our services to them in their environment. They can either come and get it or go to hell. The choice is theirs, and it's no concern of ours." Where this occurs, it is essential for those who believe the new effort is important to associate themselves into an independent sponsoring group without seeking the approval of others. They may have to put some of their church gifts to this task; they will have to give their time to the undertaking and give the rest of the church a good demonstration of an experimental effort at ministry to an estranged population. Hopefully, this kind of effort can be attempted without the necessity to create bitter conflict in the life of a congregation. But these efforts must be made regardless of conflict or opposition.

In other situations persons who see the necessity of new forms of work in the community will band together across the lines of congregations, denominations, and faiths. They will see the problem similarly and so will take the best ecumenical posture and associate themselves with anyone else who wants to join in on the undertaking. In such efforts it may be wise to seek counsel from an attorney regarding the possibility of incorporating the group in order to assure contributors of tax exemptions for their contributions. By establishing a nonprofit corporation, you will be able to receive gifts from other sources such as foundations and other churches, and assure them of responsible handling of such funds.

One of the best places for lodging experimental ministries is with an ecumenical group of cosponsors. They can jointly plan, fund, staff, and conduct such a ministry. Each will serve as a check on the other to avoid premature discouragement, provide a broader base of support and a wider range of personnel from which to select the advisory body.

Today we are experiencing a resurgence of the fundamental pietistic stance in the church. It is triggered by the fact that the wave of commitment toward redefinition of the church's role in human affairs has begun to be effective. More clergy and laity are clearly committed to renewal and redefinition. The backlash has begun. The conservative forces are not opposing the renewal movement on the theological issues of renewal. Rather, they are trying to enforce their concept of piety on all churchmen. This can be seen quite clearly in The United Methodist Church. There is a growing body of Methodists, both lay and clerical, who do not hold with the abstinent position in matters of alcohol. Most are related to the renewal movement. From 1964 to 1968 clergy were required to take a vow of abstinence from alcohol on entry to the denomination. But many committees forgot to ask the question or approved the candidate regardless of his answer. The very people who established guidelines were reluctant to enforce them. Other illustrations might be drawn from other confessions.

What this says to the renewal movement is that we must listen carefully to those who make charges against us. But we must not believe that every barking dog will bite. Nor must we believe that there is no danger. Many persons will be attacked and hurt in the transition years which we are now entering, some with little justification. The renewalists must make provision for those who receive the wrath and sting of the fundamental backlash.

One thing is sure: the new generation wants to meet a churchman who can be logical, informed, self-confident, courageous, and venturesome. Young adults aren't impressed with a pietistic life style that says "No! No!" to this or that without logical reasons established from experience. The juice of the grape, the discovery of sex, the company of others unlike us, the love of self, the freedom of the mind and the spirit are all good things, and no amount of naysaying will convince them otherwise. To refuse to know these things, to continue to say no to them, will result in our being labeled phony, and our contact will have ended— rightly so!

In spite of the dangers from within the church and the difficulties to be expected from the generation, it is time to try. Those who believe that a new possibility lies out there must act now.

BEING WITH AND AMONG THEM

The major reason for the distance between the generations is our negligence in participating with the new generation people on their terms. We have isolated ourselves from their experiences. We neither know, understand, nor feel the impact of experiences which are shaping this new generation. We are seldom with them except when they come to us. Nothing significant will be changed in the trend toward estrangement between us unless we are ready to be with and among this generation. We must spend time, lots of time, with them. We must become students of their world. We must give ourselves to learning what they perceive, feel, and conclude about life today.

This necessity to be with young adults is not a plan to go native. There is no need to take on every aspect of their behavior, their styles, their language. It is not necessary for us to join their movements and ways to be accepted by them. Almost any culture has the capacity to accept a person with different style and behavior, so long as that person makes a serious attempt to accept and understand the way of life of that culture. If that person seems willing to join the natives in trying to resolve their most difficult problems, he is apt to become an influential part of their life or community, even though he functions from a different frame of reference. For years white missionaries were accepted in black tribes. Western men have been accepted in Oriental culture. And here in America, we "straight" people can be accepted in the new generation culture if we are willing to try.

Everyone trying to understand the hippies needn't acquire sandals, long hair, beads, and buttons. What he must do is become completely familiar with hippies as persons, talking and working with them on matters that concern them. Many of the people who are today bridging the gap between the generations generally appear in white collars and ties. But they do genuinely care about the welfare of the hippie community in their city. The same thing is true of our relationships to college students, young military personnel, vocational school students, and others.

Here is where our intentions come into the picture again. If we go to their world to be observers, sitting on the sidelines making cute remarks to one another, we can expect to get the silent treatment. We must be committed not only to learning on their grounds and from them, but we must be prepared to follow through whenever we discover an issue that causes them unfair or unjust treatment by other forces in our adult culture.

A few years ago a young clergyman attempting an experimental work among young adults discovered that a great many young adults in his city were a part of the homophile world. He counseled with his advisory board, and they agreed that he should study the life experience of homosexuals. He slowly gained their confidence and respect as a clergyman who was genuinely concerned about their second-class status in the city and its institutions. As time progressed, the minister became a highly trusted confidant. He became one to whom leaders in the homophile population turned for counsel and friendship. One day a telephone call reported that a gay bar had been closed by the Alcoholic Beverage Control Board. The owner-manager was a responsible leader in the homophile community. He felt he had been forced to close unjustly. He called to ask the clergyman, the one who had been representing himself as a friend concerned about justice and dignity, if he would intervene by asking the Control Board to restore his liquor license. The clergyman was a Methodist whose parent body opposed use of alcoholic beverages. What was he to do? Could he say, "If your problem were something else, I'd really be concerned, but . . ." ? Could he say that, though he had pretended genuine concern for justice and other values, he really couldn't go to bat for the bar owner in this instance? After a careful investigation, the minister concluded that the owner had been a victim of a deliberate police trap. He went to his friend, and after joint consultation they chose a course of action. The clergyman wrote the letter of protest and asked that the decision be reversed, that the license to serve liquor be restored.

When we offer friendship, we must be prepared to take some shaking consequences. Friendships are important, and with the new generation they are the key to a climate of trust and mutual respect. Whenever one goes into the young adult world, he must be sure of his intentions. If he goes only to look and learn, then he had better not try to pretend he cares. Most of the subcultures of our national life are full of real problems which are often bigger than the subculture can handle alone. Adults who seem willing to act as bridges will be given the opportunity.

In his paper called "The Identification of Mission by

Penetration," my friend and former colleague Ted McIlvenna shares eight simple guidelines which for him form such a methodology for identifying mission. They are:

1. I simply went wherever there were people congregating. I have saturated myself with the city. Wherever young adults went . . . there I went, too.
2. I learned to identify with "urban men." This was really easy for I found him very like myself.
3. I enjoyed myself.
4. I tried not to be a phony human being. . . . I never pretended to be anything else than what I am. At no point did I feel it necessary to defend the church emotionally.
5. I learned to be quiet. I learned to listen.
6. I learned to ask questions and then to take the answers seriously.
7. I learned to recognize my own limitations and not to pretend that I was an expert. I learned to recognize valid commitments of other people. I discovered the need to rely on others for guidance and learned that the guidance I needed came only when I was able to establish a valid relationship with them in the sharing of a common commitment.
8. I forced myself to go places where I was frightened to go. When I got there I found that I was more often than not caught up in the action.[1]

This is the essence of the doctrine of incarnation! The church must put persons into situations where they can enact the role and work of missioners, not because we can live there better but rather because we can find the key to our own life only by discovering the key to more abundant life for others—in this case, the new generation.

For those who claim to care will surely be called on to demonstrate the extent of their caring. To demonstrate the extent of our caring goes far beyond all words. To run from such action also speaks louder than all our words. When we go to learn about and care for others, we will be put to the test.

DISCOVERY OF MISSION

Most churches are aware of young adults, familiar with old approaches that either fail or have only limited response. What they do not have is a clear sense of what they are being called to do with and about the current young adult population. This being *with* them is more than an education. It is more than being tested. It is the best means available to identify the critical issues they are facing. To know the problems a people face is the foundation of mission in the midst of that people. For the young black, the problem is rights and opportunity. For the young male, the problem is the inevitability of being a part of what is rapidly becoming a very unpopular war machine.

By living among others, we discover where they hurt. We began to know in what areas and on what issues they long to hear something that has the sound of good news. We discover where they are afraid, where they are courageous, where they are overwhelmed, where they need support from beyond their own sources. We have long believed that the hungry plea of a beggar was God's call for us to be generous. By living among the new generation, we will learn what causes them to cry out with pain, with despair, with frustration, with anger and hate. Only when we discover these signs of suffering will we discover our calling in their midst.

eight

The Church Can Help_____

Form follows function. This must be the guideline for the church to improve its relationship with the new generation. The task is one of creativity and innovation. It is an undertaking of study, listening, incorporating new information and new perceptions into our thinking. It is a task to be done cooperatively. We must acknowledge our interdependence with the new generation. What we each become in the next decade is a common issue. At times the new generation will be our teachers.

We are entering a new era in the history of the Christian movement. Earlier transition periods resulted in new forms for the church. There will be a major decline and considerable conflict within the church. The era we are approaching is as significant as was the decision for a mission to the gentiles by the first disciples, the nationalization of faith by Constantine, the emergence of the local church as a congregational form in the tenth century, the Protestant Reformation, and the era of sectarianism through which we are now passing.

The new era will be characterized by an ecumenical spirit which manifests itself in an ever-growing process of church union. The same spirit will bring the major faith movements of the world into much closer relationship. It will result in the Christian churches and peoples being much more concerned about and involved in the events that affect the welfare of human beings in this life, here and now. The church will attempt to develop increased power in political decisions, drawing on the resources of moral persuasion, organization of the underprivileged or victims of injustice, infiltration of the political, economic, and governmental structures of the society, not to take over but to influence the kind of questions and issues which are placed on the agenda of the nations, the cities, the corporations, and the parties.

We must discern *functions* which have worth to the new generation and which we have the resources and will to fulfill. If Marshall McLuhan is correct, adequately enacted functions will in and of themselves represent the message which the church has for this new generation. We must witness through our functioning. If we have something to say about love, then it must be said through loving. If we carry a word about justice, then it must be said through opposing injustice and fighting for justice.

141

INTERPRETERS

Historically, Christians have believed that every person is of worth. We have believed that every man and woman deserves to be treated with respect and dignity. Our biblical sources teach us that all men have faults, and one must be careful about the way he responds to those who differ from himself. Two good examples from the biblical accounts are Jesus' admonition to the crowd about to stone the prostitute and his teaching about the mote and the beam.

These new generation people are different. They have been watched, criticized, and judged by just about everyone. Frequently, I read a report on an event about which I happen to have personal information, and I am startled with the amount of misinformation which is reported, even by major magazines, news services, and television media. What the church is called to do is to attempt to supply correct information about any such error. When misinformation and opinionated, negative interpretation of events and behavior are as widespread as in the case of the new generation, we must devise ways to take the initiative with corrective interpretations.

AFFIRMATION

Our problem is that the church leadership often knows so little about the generation that it cannot evaluate the accuracy of what it hears or reads. An improved witness with the new generation depends on whether we will be with them enough to know them, their life experiences, and their world views. Unbiased, objective, and sympathetic interpretation is needed. The church can provide this interpretive function if it is willing to become sufficiently involved to have an adequate understanding. For any church group to undertake this function means it must go be with the generation and sustain a constant dialogue about what is happening to and among its members. There are constant stories of police harassment and brutality, of discrimination in public services such as health programs, housing codes, inadequate educational offerings from colleges and universities, poor apartment and housing services, inadequate transportation services, and there is a great need for help in living in a modern city. There must be a constant struggle to arrange ways by which the new generation can receive a fair hearing on the matters which concern them. Few officials want to listen to them, for they are neither voters nor big taxpayers. But they are citizens; and, more important, they are human beings, and their welfare should rightly be *our* concern. They are our sons and daughters, our nieces and nephews, grandsons and granddaughters.

When the church is adequately informed and is ready to speak out in behalf of a fair hearing or just treatment for the members of this new generation, we will be much closer to gaining their respect. For we have preached these things to them as children and youth, but to do them will be the clear witness that we, the church, have the potential of bearing good news to them and their generation. It will be love enacted. Good news must be acted out in the specifics of each local community and neighborhood. One way to begin is by being informed, able interpreters of the generation.

Example: The Glide Urban Center, a church urban program, has recently put its long involvement with the hippie culture in San Francisco into a small book titled *Hippie Is Necessary.*[1] The book provides our society with an interpretation of the hippie culture and movement which is not available elsewhere. It is a report which acquires its authority through extensive involvement preceding its publication. The book was not written after two or three days' visiting in San Francisco and talking to a few hippies. It is the result of years of close, sustained ties with leaders and others in the hippie population. It clearly reports hippie culture as it is. It recognizes that the hippie movement has many worthwhile dimensions. It affirms much, though not all, that occurs in this unique new generation population.

Example: The National Young Adult Project, in cooperation with several Protestant denominations, has released a film, *Could You Answer My Question?* which provides a portrayal of much of the life of this new generation. It interprets its life styles and behaviors without judging them as wrong just because they differ from the predominant thinking of our day. The film affirms much that happens through the initiative of the new generation and calls for the church to increase involvement with and awareness of the new generation.[2]

Example: In Dallas, Texas, a local group of churchmen sponsors a series of Exposure Programs. It takes small groups of churchmen over a period of several weeks, exposing them to the different kinds of people in the city. Several sessions deal primarily with the new generation. The program has two meetings weekly: one provides an interpretation and discussion with persons from some subculture in the city, and the other is actual confrontation with persons in that same subculture on their grounds and in their own places. Through this process churchmen are becoming sensitive to the problems and perceptions of people different from themselves. A participant leaves the Exposure experience better qualified to be an interpreter who has seen "the other side" of the issues affecting people in Dallas.

SENSORY EFFORT THROUGH SIGNIFICANT PERSONS

Erik Erikson introduces the concept of the "adult guarantor" in his discussion of the experiences which assist persons to mature into able, confident adults. Ross Snyder of Chicago Theological Seminary has done considerable work on this concept and defines it as the existence of a relationship between a younger person and an older person in which the older becomes a kind of guaranteeing symbol that the discovery of meanings in life is worth the effort. Thus, the adult guarantor.

Ted McIlvenna, coming at the needs of the new generation from a social rather than a psychological perspective, concludes that every young adult needs frequent contact and firsthand friendship with socially aware adults. He is calling for adults who are concerned about the critical social issues of the day to make their concern known to the younger generation through face-to-face contacts with them. He is saying that young adults must know that there are people in the adult society who approach life in a probing fashion, willing to take stands where needed. These adults could join in the movements of the new generation to identify and oppose the social ills adversely affecting the new generation in the cities and the nation.

This need for contacts with significant adult persons may

be an area in which the church can develop a ministry. We must look for our most socially sensitive and self-confident people and ask them to make themselves available for frequent contacts with members of the new generation. These contacts will be demonstrative of our concern. They should occur on the young adult's ground and on his terms.

Unfortunately, many of the contacts the new generation has with the adult churchman are with the ultraconservatives. These often represent a gross indifference to the social problems the young adult is experiencing and a disproportionate desire to "save" *him* from the world. They oppose much of the young adult life style because it does not fit the monolithic view they have about life. They are critical, judgmental, and insensitive to the young adult's immediate problems. They do not want to be a part of his life. They want him to deny himself and his peers and become a part of their group.

If the churches in the more open traditions can carefully select adults who are mature, who symbolize that life is worth living, who care enough about human experience that they will join the new generation in working on some of *their* problems, we will have begun an effort which will far outweigh all the sermons we preach. This enacting of our friendship, our caring, our interdependence with them can be a breakthrough. I do not suggest that we will immediately be accepted, given recognition, or come home with a band of followers. No, hardly that! We will find that it is slow going at first. Rejection will be frequent. Those who go in this role must go prepared to stick it out, seeking a place of acceptance after they have proved their intentions.

146

Young adults who turn to the church with some regularity also need to know significant people personally. They need opportunities to meet such people, so that they may discover one or two with whom they can establish a sustained relationship.

Example: A church which has several young adults coming to its various activities schedules frequent opportunities for key community leaders to spend an evening or weekend with the young adults in informal settings. Everyone is simply himself. No programs to conduct, no schedule to cling to . . . just opportunity to know one another and explore those things which are mutually important.

Example: A number of churches operate weekend coffeehouses to which they regularly invite significant adults to be available for talk with anyone on any issue. These guests do not need to be persons with prestigious church positions. They may not be churchmen at all. The important thing is that the church has the ability and the desire to put the new generation in touch with significant people whom it could not know otherwise. It communicates a desire for openness and an understanding of early adulthood which will be appreciated. The new generation's response will usually be affirmative. When affirmative responses occur, the good news has been heard and recognized, either in words or in actions.

Example: Almost every church has a few members who are extremely active in numerous social action groups. These people, while members of the church, are frequently marginal in their participation. They often feel that the church doesn't really want them around. They feel that the church doesn't acknowledge their action orientation as the behavior of good churchmen. For truly they would rather go to a social action meeting than any church meeting.

In relating to the new generation, these persons are often the best qualified. They are active, involved, courageous, and they have repeatedly taken stands on critical issues. They actually know many young adults, for most of the manpower of the social action groups today is composed of young adults. These persons who have been what we called marginal members now become one of the keys to the door to the new generation. The church must view these persons as a kind of sensory task force who know what is happening among several types of young adults. They are with the new generation in its causes, its hopes and dreams, and also its disappointment, suffering, and defeat. They know what has meaning to the new generation. They know the new generation people. They are sharing life together. The church can give strong support to those who have been taking this role. It can call on these people to provide perspectives, perceptions, and other data to define and portray the new generation more accurately. More important, the church can send others to join these who already work in this area. Significant adults are needed everywhere. But we remember that there is a great difference between warm bodies and significant adults.

CONTEXUAL COUNSELOR

In the mid-sixties I coordinated three action-research projects, each of which attempted to test quite different assumptions regarding the church's ministry among young

adults. When completed, each experience led to the conclusion that there is an immense need for extended and
improved counseling services. The generation is in the
transition from youth toward adulthood, and the various
developmental aspects of this transition require assistance
for many of them. They are in transition from parental
dependence to independence. They are learning new truths
which often conflict with earlier assumptions, opinions, or
views. They are discovering that the world is full of con-
flicts and disagreements. They are learning to work with
others, to share living accommodations, to deal with social
and personal problems ranging from sex to money.

It is still assumed in our society that, when one has a
problem, it may be desirable to talk it over with a clergyman. Counseling is the one field of human services in which
the church has not been overshadowed by government
or private undertakings. Each of the directors of the several
projects concluded that he could have spent all his time in
counseling situations.

Directors found a much larger demand on their time
for counseling than the average clergyman. Though there
was no attempt to document the reason for this, it may have
been due to the way they were totally immersed in the
young adult culture. They were seen wherever the new
generation went. They established their interest and concern by their presence, not by some oral or mimeographed
announcement. The great majority of the counseling situations developed because the directors had become known
to care about the young adults in their city.

The directors' regular involvement in the issues which
affected young adults was often the reason young persons

gave for seeking their counsel. For example, when it became known that someone was conducting a study of the housing conditions in which many young adults had to live, calls began to come asking help in finding adequate housing or getting facilities brought up to code, or reporting violations of the code and wanting advice on what to do about such things. When it became known that the directors were working on the problems of unwed mothers and unwanted children, calls came asking for sources of birth control information, where abortions could be secured, how pressure could be brought on irresponsible men who had fathered an expected child, how to place a child for adoption, sources of medical services when there was no money for a doctor in private practice, and a host of related questions.

The other factor which seems to be similar in these projects was that the project directors all were able to discuss the person's problem in its *context*. They did not begin their counseling with open and closed answers to personal problems. At times they could counsel that an abortion was the best choice. In other cases they urged that the person seriously explore marriage or else have the child with the intention of placing the child with an adoption agency. Whether it was with sex, alcohol, marriage problems, family problems, questions of war, peace, the draft, drugs, education, employment, these men were prepared to handle the problem in a way which provided maximum review of the factors related to the problem and a specific conclusion for each situation. They didn't carry a bag of simple absolutes and patch one on here and another there. They knew enough about the issues at hand to know that each situation deserved a specific answer according to the circumstances.

This ability to examine one's problems contextually is an urgent need. Churches could assist greatly in this area if they would be prepared to put the person and his problem first and discard the usual tendency to have an answer ready before the question is asked. That rigid absolutist approach to counseling is generally not helpful. It becomes a form which further alienates the new generation from the church.

Example: Some churches have full-time or part-time professional counselors on their staff. These persons can become a useful force in bridging the generation gap if they will plan their time so that they may become more involved with the life experience of the new generation. They need to be seen by young adults when they are about town, involved in some service or protest. This is an important aspect of service to younger persons. These adults should involve themselves in young adult issues. Out of this involvement will come contacts which will lead to counseling situations.

Example: Some churches already conduct group therapy sessions in which young adults are participating. Occasionally there is a group specifically for young adults. However, it may be more desirable to have young adults mixed into groups representing a wider age and experience span. Thus, when young men or women come to the church and it is obvious that they have personal problems, they can identify with one of these groups. Such groups must be conducted by competent persons who know what they are doing. Most larger churches have such persons in the membership, and it might be possible to secure their services in such a ministry. Many pastors have professional training in this field.

Moreover, we can often recognize the need for a service such as this and use our influence to get appropriate agencies to provide the needed services. Many times the church concludes that, if it cannot meet the need, there is nothing to do. When we accept the principle that form follows function, then the crucial first step is to identify needed functions. The second step is to devise a suitable form of response. Here is were we need a good, healthy view of the world. We must recognize that others may be better equipped to provide the response. They may have the money, facilities, professional personnel, etc., to respond far more helpfully than any response the church could manage.

On particular issues government agency services may have to be supplemented. Sometimes they are bound by antiquated laws which limit the range of their services. For example, many state family planning agencies cannot provide comprehensive advice or information on birth control. So sometimes we must examine the context in which a problem exists and supply the missing elements of an adequate response.

Example: There is such a large demand for counseling on every conceivable subject that the idea of a counseling center specifically for young adults has been proposed, though to my knowledge none is yet in operation. It would operate at the hours when young adults are free, namely, late evenings and weekends. For example, it might open around 4:00 P.M. and close at midnight on week nights and remain open twenty-four hours a day from Friday at 4:00 P.M. through Sunday midnight. The schedule would depend on local factors. Such a center, staffed by persons who were required to spend at least one evening every week involved in young adult affairs, would quickly become known; and, if the contextual approach to problem solving were used, it would provide a monumental service.

Note: The need for counseling could consume every possible person. But there are other services to be provided in behalf of and with the new generation. When other services are the intention of an individual or a group, strong discipline will have to be exercised to avoid being drawn into the role of full-time counselor(s).

THE ENABLING FUNCTION

When we decide the new generation is worth loving and worth living for, the church can assume the role of enabler to much of the young adults' own dreams and hopes. An enabler is one who helps another accomplish something which is the latter's goal. The enabler does not take over. He does not assume credit for the accomplishment. He simply shares in accomplishing the intended goal. An enabler is what a parent is to a child about to take his first step. The parent has walked the baby, coaxed, encouraged, and watched him fall, only to give the encouragement to try again. But, when the child walks, it is *his* accomplishment. The enabler is concerned for the accomplishment, not the credit.

The new generation people have important things they want to accomplish. They may be limited in the resources necessary to fulfill that desire. The church often has more resources than it uses wisely. We often find ourselves spending enormous sums on extravagant things because we have become so out of touch with people who have dreams and hopes but limited resources. Our resources include our financial accounts, buildings, lawns, parking lots, adjacent properties, members who hold strategic positions in the city, our staff, the equipment such as kitchens, audiovisual equipment, our printing or mimeograph facilities, church mailings, and so on.

We are so limited by our attitude that we must first judge and approve everything before we help. If the church could develop the self-image and maturity that are exercised by the news networks, we would be in a position to perform the enabling function. We can allow many things to happen without having to be fully in accord with them. The news media give time, coverage, and freedom to individuals and groups without feeling that their reputation hangs on whether what is being reported concurs with the position of the management of the network. We must learn to assist people in accomplishing their goals whether we are always in complete agreement or not. To *enable* another to do what he is compelled to do is good news to him. Obviously some discretion is required but, I suspect, much less than the "fear" or "holier-than-thou" attitudes which currently prevail.

Example: A church allows various groups of new generation people to have unrestricted access to their duplicating equipment. They have made it clear that the use of their equipment does not in any way represent endorsement of the content of the material. The groups who prepare the material and distribute it must take sole responsibility for it. Any printing shop operates on the same basis. When they are given access to a means of distributing their ideas, young persons discover that, whether we agree or disagree, we believe there is room in the world for them. That kind of affirmation of persons goes much farther in communicating love and respect for human beings than sermons and lessons.

Example: In one city a neighborhood had suddenly shifted to a major young adult area. Many of the newcomers were not eating regularly because they were unemployed and without adequate food. A small group of young adults took it upon themselves to get together enough food to serve one free hot meal a day to those who wanted it. But soon scores were coming. The group didn't give up, even though finding that much food, or money for food, was now a major undertaking. A church in the neighborhood heard about their project, offered them the use of its fully equipped kitchen in which to prepare the food. That church was an enabler. Caring of this kind could not be matched by words.

Example: A group of young adults discovered that welfare mothers received only a five-dollar allotment to buy school clothing for their children each year. They organized the mothers in a protest march on a local department store. But where would they form the march? A downtown church opened its doors as a meeting and starting place for the march. The church cared about the issues of endorsing people who are trying to face difficult situations.

Example: Several churches in one city took a broad look at their young adult population. They employed a man to represent their interest in and support of the new generation. He was not to organize church groups but to find out what young adults were doing and what they wanted to do and help them accomplish their own goals, thus affirming their own worth, dignity, and dreams.

Note: The enabling role is not performed without deliberate assessment of the consequences of each situation. Occasionally we will find a group who will try to take advantage of our interest. I suppose that is why we have been counseled to be wise as serpents! But if we are to have any breakthrough with the new generation, we must get into the midst of their action. We haven't been advised to be as cautious as cowards or as inactive as sloths!

Example: I have been in numerous cities where young churchmen saw little significance in the life and practice they found in local churches. They believed that the Christian way of life held the key to their own self-understanding and the style of life they wanted to live. They sought a chance to begin with the basic functions of Christian living and redefine the *forms* through which those *functions* could be expressed most appropriately for their generation.

These young people generally want to establish a living group which will define and fulfill the nature of Christian living being called for in their age. Unfortunately, more often than not, this plea falls on deaf ears. Some churches see it as a rejection of them, and sometimes it is, because the forms in those churches have become irrelevant to the new generation's experience. It then becomes evident that we have come to love our present forms more than the functions. We have put our love for the church above our faithfulness to Jesus' spirit. Other churches want to take the idea of living groups but put so many conditions on it that no freedom is left in which to define any creative forms of faithfulness. Only rarely has such a group had a chance to try this experiment. Most of the few that have occurred have been in relation to campus ministries. Leaders of such enabling groups are to be commended. The young men and women who have had opportunity to attempt this approach to a Christian life style seem almost universally appreciative for the chance. They have, through this opportunity, discovered the difficulty of making appropriate faithful responses to the complex issues of our age.

We must now expect our larger congregations and our regional associations such as synods, presbyteries, dioceses, districts, and conferences to support such groups of young churchmen. We should provide them with facilities, freedom, and the resources they need to be these experimental communities of young Christians in mission.

DEALING WITH ISSUES

The most articulate, perceptive, aggressive persons of the new generation seem to be caught up in dealing with critical issues of the day. The church's best opportunity to be with the new generation is around current issues. The young Americans are undoubtedly more issue oriented than their predecessors at the same time of life.

The church must ally itself with the emerging new generation movements. These movements deal with issues of freedom, peace, voice, and services. They are loosely knit, strangely organized, and one sometimes wonders if they even exist. But they do exist, and they do attract the sympathy of thousands of young adults who will never be at any of their meetings or demonstrations. For example, the number of young men and women who will join an antiwar demonstration in Nashville, Tennessee, will number little more than one hundred—a generous figure! But when a teach-in occurs on the campus of one of its universities concerning hawks versus the antiwar voice, thousands come to cheer those who lead in the antiwar demonstrations. And ten thousand turned out on a rainy night to affirm Robert Kennedy's goal to change the war policies of the nation. They perceive the importance of the issue, and they are ready to dissent.

The new generation seems to focus attention on two kinds of issues: those that radically affect the future, such as war policies and participatory democracy, and those that immediately affect the young adult's finding a place in our contemporary society, such as housing or education.

If the church is to make any significant strides toward overcoming the generation gap, we will have to identify ourselves seriously with the movements that seek reform of policies related to such issues.

These issues have been identified and referred to throughout the preceding material.

Example: Several years ago a group of churchmen and homosexuals met to discuss the problems related to being homosexual in our American culture. Out of this study of the issue came the formation of the first Council on Religion and the Homosexual, an organization whose purpose was to further education about and understanding of the aspects of homosexuality and to promote more equal acceptance of homosexuals in the full spectrum of our life. Its membership was drawn from the male and female homosexual communities and from the churches, both lay and clergy.

Many young citizens, not *gay* themselves, have close

friends who are. The *straight* world is getting a more sensitive education in the problems, experiences, and realities of life for the homosexual. They are discovering that the civil rights of homosexuals are denied. Local police departments do send young officers, dressed in tight-fitting civilian clothing, into bars where homosexuals go in a deliberate attempt to "pick up" a homosexual person. As soon as they do, other police officers arrest the latter and file a "morals" charge against him. The homosexual is often denied jobs for which he is fully competent for no reason except his sexual orientation. He is often dismissed from jobs which he is performing with full competency simply because someone has discovered that he is a homosexual. He is often denied access to housing and is always denied the right to serve in the armed forces and in many instances receives less than a "fair shake" before courts because someone assumes that being homosexual is, in and of itself, incriminating and illegal.

We keep statutes in all fifty states that are obsolete and ridiculous in light of current knowledge about homosexuality. Our laws, without exception, provide that practicing homosexual acts is a social crime. Newer, enlightened laws, such as the British Parliament passed in 1967, are needed.

The original consultation was held under the auspices of the National Young Adult Project, a religious effort to bridge the gap between the new generation and the church. Since homosexuality is a problem which looms largest among the young, it came forth as an issue to be faced. Since that time several chapters of CRH have been organized in the United States and Canada. One major denomination sees the urgency of relating to the issues and contributes several hundred dollars annually to the operating budget of the parent chapter of CRH.

The significance of the church's relating to this issue is that the homophile population (some estimate as high as eighteen million) has seen the church take the first serious effort to affirm its life situation rather than judge it. Homosexuals have seen the church acting out of a genuine concern to know and understand them and their world. They have perceived the church as caring, an attitude hard to find earlier. They have a new view toward the church; there is more openness, and much more accurate information is being passed through the dialogues that now occur, replacing old stereotypes and distorted information.

Example: In Miami, Florida, students of the Miami-Dade Junior College (now with over 26,000 students) are given no assistance from the college in finding living facilities. It is more and more difficult to find adequate housing as the number of students grows. Rates are high, since students must compete with winter vacationers for rooming space. The Miami Young Adult Ministry, Inc. (MYAMI) has established a housing finder service for students. It works on one end of the problem by trying to urge families and others to make rooms available to students, and at the other end it locates students in these facilities. Now labeled as "mini-HUD," it is preparing for its second year of dealing helpfully with the housing issue affecting these students.

Example: Many young adults coming to larger cities for the first time find that they are overwhelmed by the size, sound, neon, hustle, coldness, and anonymity of the city. Learning to live there becomes a crucial issue. In various cities urban orientation centers have been established to

160

assist in this problem. Sometimes called Gateway, the centers make available information on employment, housing, travel, organizations, movements, legal services, health services, welfare services, as well as a chance for young adults to work in Gateway itself as volunteers, thereby meeting other young adults facing similar experiences. These centers have been significantly utilized by the new generation people. However, the church has yet to take this kind of ministry seriously enough to establish and maintain such centers except for short periods of time.

Example: The artists of the new generation are currently making an immeasurable impact on our whole society. For example, the art of the hippie movement has now influenced the clothing that men and women purchase at Sears! These young artists need outlets for their talent. They need a forum where their creations can be tested. They need a place to read their poetry, sing their songs, hang their art, act out their drama, make their sounds, and, in general, "do their thing." In Dallas, Satori House is such a center, funded and opened by a church group and staffed by young generation artists. The Satori House group performed at the Hemisfair in San Antonio in 1968 because of the exposure which it gained from the ministry of Satori House. The church provides a forum, a spotlight, a visible place, and in so doing demonstrates a genuine concern for these new generation artists and their work. They know the church cares, and in knowing this they know a church quite different from an earlier stereotype.

_____*nine*

*Planning for Mission*_____

The effectiveness of new attempts to be in mission must
recognize rule No. 1: "Form follows function." The recent
history of experimental ministries has produced a host of
forms. Some have been in business for a long time, while
others have opened and closed almost immediately. The
important question is, what makes the difference? Why do
some succeed and others fail? What is the key to success?
The clue to success lies first in function(s) and only
secondarily in form(s).

Any new experimental ministry must be born as an obedient response to fulfill some significant function of the
church's mission in the world. There must be a functional
intent to any ministry. What function is required because of

the situation to which you want to respond? Can the church be more obedient by doing it?

The diagram on page 164 may help in the process of developing function-centered responses.

STEPS IN PLANNING FOR MISSION

The seedbed for any response by the church today, as always, is in the needs of the human experience. This premise is easily identified in the actions which are recorded in the New Testament and attributed to the work Jesus did. He responded to situations of human need. In some cases it was the need or problem of one individual; in others it was a problem of many. Whenever Jesus interpreted what he was doing, it was clear that he was living his life for all men in need everywhere. Any faithful response of contemporary Christians lies in the sensitivity to the crises of human experience today in the ghettos, the mountains, the reservations, the farms, and the suburbs.

In spite of the sincerity of the national structures of the churches, the programs they promote may or may not be what formulates an appropriate and obedient response to the needs, problems, and issues which affect the people surrounding a given church, city, or region. When these programs do meet the need, they are helpful. When they do not meet the need, we must set them aside without hesitation. Our obedience is measured by our response to the existing needs and problems. We are not measured by our loyalty to a national board, regional agency or conference, synod, diocese, presbytery, district package program.

One of the hopeful signs is to see national agencies developing guidelines recognizing that the agency is not

STEPS IN PLANNING FOR MISSION

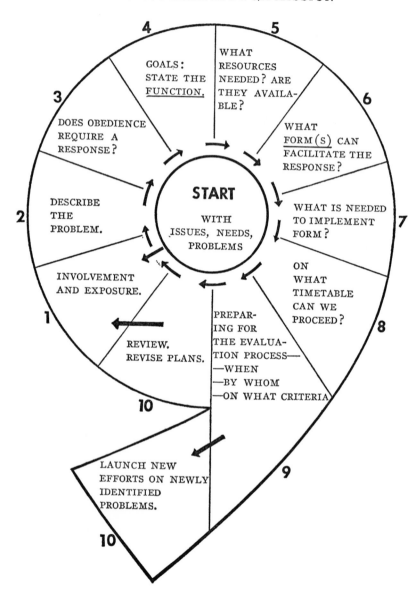

called upon to tell the whole church what it should be doing. These same agencies are recognizing that faithfulness lies in obedience of local response to local problems. There are also national problems which exist throughout all local areas, and it is appropriate for the national agency to undertake leadership in an appropriate response to such situations. However, national agencies must not neglect to assist and stand with local people. In so doing they are made aware of the kind and extent of local problems. Mission planning must be centered on people and their problems. (Note the circle at core of the diagram.)

1. Exposure to the local problem is essential. We are required to be faithful. We are not endowed with magical wisdom and power. Until we have set ourselves in the midst of a problem and allowed it to eat its way into who we are as human beings, we are in no condition to propose any response. Committees with good intentions and no firsthand involvement in the problem they are considering should go home and forget it. Chances are they will not do anything of real worth.

Exposure can be gained from making contact with someone who is in the midst of the particular issue or problem. Make known your own interest in the problem and your lack of accurate information and awareness. Ask for help to learn the realities surrounding the problem. Ask for help to probe the problem. Ask to be introduced to others who know the problem in a firsthand way. Keep asking everyone you meet, "Who else should I talk to?" Stay at it until you begin to find a wide spectrum of viewpoints about the cause and solution of the problem. Stay at it long enough to discover that certain facts, attitudes, elements of the problem seem to be recurring in your interviews and contacts. Write down what you learn. Systematize your information.

2. As you maintain your contacts within the problem area, start working on a definitive statement of the problem, its present effect, extent, and also its causes. What effect is it having on individuals, neighborhoods, the whole section of the public who experience it? How deeply is it embedded into the stream of life of the city? Why has it gone unchallenged, unchanged? What are the main elements of the problem? Are there ways they can be approached so as to change, correct them? What kinds of changes will have to be accomplished in order to make a difference in the very nature of the problem as it now exists? Who are the key people who will be helpful to you? Who are the people who are going to be the "enemy"?

3. In light of your study and involvement, does obedience to the Christian faith require an attempt to deal with this issue? Is this a genuine problem affecting the quality of life of people? Is it the kind of problem which deserves your attention?

4. What is it that we are required to do about this situation? Here is a very pivotal step in the process. This is the time when there must be clarified the *function* being called for. This will become the base on which everything ahead will be measured. Work on this step must be clear, mutually agreed upon, and stated very precisely. A statement of function might begin with a phrase such as:

> *In order to be faithful to our Christian commitment, in the midst of this problem, the church must do the following things:*

Be sure to state them in terms of function, not forms. For

example, don't list a coffeehouse as one of the things to be done. If the desire is for increasing the dialogue among people affected by the problem, then list the function in that way. Later, when you get to the point of forms, you may decide that the best environment of open dialogue is a coffeehouse, but hold all questions of form until there is clarity of function. Functional statements become the guidelines on which you will be able to decide to what extent you have succeeded or failed. Without good work on functions you will be without guidelines for evaluation and long-range planning. These functional statements become the goals or objectives of the proposed mission.

5. Once you have stated your functions and goals, you must then ask a very realistic question. What resources are required to fulfill this function? The crucial resources to be identified here include (1) the availability of persons with expertise in the various aspects of the proposed functions, (2) the extent of support and acceptance the function can get from your organization, (3) the contacts available to "sell the idea" to strategic persons, (4) adequate entry points through which to relate directly to the problem, and (5) a level of commitment from a hard core of persons who are prepared to see the proposal through. In this way you are testing the feasibility of further action.

6. In what *form* can the response be made? Rule No. 2: Form must match function. Work on form prior to this must be kept to a minimum in order not to short-circuit the more basic planning in regard to problem, function, and feasibility. Now is the time to ask, if we want dialogue to occur, what format can we use to encourage and allow it to happen? The answer might be a coffeehouse or a forum or

neighborhood meetings or something else. The importance of finding a form which maximizes the possibility that the desired function will happen cannot be overstressed. A planning group should never latch onto the first form that is suggested without further examination. The most useful forms generally emerge through a process in which planners suggest a number of alternative forms and then compare the advantages and disadvantages of each, choosing the one that offers the best possibilities for success.

7. When a form has been chosen, the planners must assess "what will be required to implement it." What kind of money, contacts, tools, equipment, persons, planning, staffing, etc., will be required to utilize this idea for form? There is a tendency on the part of many church groups to be less than realistic at this point. Most church groups feel they must operate on a pennies-and-nickels approach, borrow or beg facilities, take whatever is cheap and available, use volunteer helpers, collect surplus and unwanted equipment and tools. No doubt much effective work has occurred through imaginative use of just such resources. There is also little doubt that many intended efforts have fallen by the way because they underestimated the strength and importance of their own idea and the way in which it could and needed to be implemented. Some forms seem to call for used facilities. Others may not. Some forms may use facilities at just any location, while others will require just the right spot or the whole function is in jeopardy. You must determine what kind, quality, and condition of tools, equipment, and facilities will help fulfill the intended function. These must somehow catch up and communicate the motif, spirit, and mystique of the desired form and

function. Actually, every decision about resources, from print to persons, is a decision about form and must be considered on the basis of whether it helps or hinders accomplishing the primary function.

8. Before starting to implement the proposed form, the planners should examine carefully the realities of timing. How long will it take to "get in business" is the overall question, but it must be answered in considerable detail. What is the date implementation procedures can begin? Tomorrow? Next week? Is there any date in the future by which it is necessary to be operating? What has to be taken care of: location, equipment, personnel, funds, interpretation, information, organizing? How long will it take for each phase? Who will be responsible for overall supervision? Who will handle each aspect of the total task? When will checkpoints be scheduled in order to assess progress and resolve complications? A good timetable will show such information as: (1) tasks to be done, (2) date to begin and finish, (3) estimate of any funds necessary, (4) persons responsible, (5) any instructions to those responsible.

9. The evaluation process must be considered at the start as well as the finish of any project. The planners must go back to the goals stated when clarifying function (step 4). These statements plus any corollaries related to testing the adequacy of the chosen form(s) provide the information from which the criteria for evaluation are drawn. Rule No. 3: Both form and function must be evaluated. A clear statement on evaluation criteria should spell out the basis on which the whole effort will be reviewed. "The project will be evaluated during the period of (dates) and criteria to be used will be: (list of criteria in question form).

The evaluation will be conducted by (name of persons or organization) in consultation with the steering group." It is helpful if an outside group can be secured to undertake the evaluation task. They must be drawn into your process early enough to gain good awareness of your intentions and experience. Such outside counsel can often identify numerous aspects of a local experience which may go unidentified by members of your own group. Evaluation done expertly is the best investment that can be made in improving the effectiveness of any given effort.

10. Review of the total experience and report of the evaluation is the final step to be undertaken. However, it is also the first step in the cycle of good planning and progress in developing good work. The central task is to identify needed changes and to put in motion these changes. Evaluation which does not direct future effort is not worth the time and energy. Generally speaking, a good evaluation report will provide clearly stated areas which need attention. It may, in some instances, make suggestions about possible solutions. It will almost always identify some new problems which have come to focus through the previous effort.

The new problems may be met through the function and form of the original effort, or they may be so different as to cause the planning group to choose clearly to avoid trying to incorporate any response to them through the existing mission. In such cases a new planning group is called for. It then starts through the cycle of steps in planning for mission with a new problem while the original group re-enters the cycle at step 1 in an effort to improve and adapt the mission according to the changes in the situation and the current possibilities of response.

The crux of planning for mission rests in these three rules: 1) *Form follows function;* 2) *form must match function;* 3) *both form and function must be evaluated.* Coffee-houses, campus centers, educational buildings, credit union offices, study halls, libraries, barracks, chapels, advisory boards, task forces, sanctuaries, pulpits, recreation halls are all forms. The function is more important than the form. Some of the above forms are now undergoing radical changes because a review of function is calling for new, imaginative, more useful forms for our time. The task of the church in mission with the new generation is just that: to develop radically new, imaginative forms which can carry the central functions of the church's mission to twentieth-century man.

Notes

1. The Big Generation

1. Edgar Z. Friedenberg, *Coming of Age in America* (New York: Random House, 1963).
2. See the *Report of the National Advisory Commission on Civil Disorders* (New York: Bantam Books, 1968), p. 466.
3. For additional information on the Council on Religion and the Homosexual write to the Council at 330 Ellis Street, San Francisco, California, 94102.
4. William O. Douglas, *A Living Bill of Rights* (Garden City, N.Y.: Doubleday, 1961), p. 33.

2. Profile of the Young Adult

1. I want to acknowledge the research which Dr. Merton Strommen of Church Youth Research has done, and the projected plans he has for additional studies which more directly focus on the young adult generation. His major contribution to date is *Profiles of Church Youth* (St. Louis: Concordia, 1963).

   Studies are also being completed at the Institute of Sex Research, more familiarly known as the Kinsey Institute, which is attempting to study the values of contemporary youth. The sample will contain both college students and peers who are not in college.
2. Muzafer Sherif and C. W. Sherif, *Problems of Youth: Transition*

to Adulthood in a Changing World (Chicago: Aldine Publishing Company, 1965), p. 21.

3. Rosemary Parks, in *Young Adults: The Threshold Years* (New York: Institute of Life Insurance, 1966), p. 32.

4. Peter C. Moore, ed., *Youth In Crisis* (New York: Seabury Press, 1966), p. 35.

5. Malcolm Knowles, address to Conference on the Laity, French Lick, Indiana, 1967.

6. Edgar Z. Friedenberg, *op. cit.*, p. 11.

7. Paul Abels, "Adolescence and Coalescence Amid the Great American Society," *Youth and Revolution*, p. 103. *Risk*, Vol. 2, no. 2 (Geneva: Youth Department of the World Council of Churches, 1966).

8. Friedenberg, *The Vanishing Adolescent* (New York: Dell Publishing Co., 1959), pp. 214-15.

9. John V. Tunney, in *Young Adults: The Threshold Years*, p. 40.

10. Michael Harrington, "The Mystical Militants," *The New Republic*, February 19, 1966, p. 20.

3. I Don't Like Church

1. Roy Larson, "Memo to a Parson, from a Wistful Young Man," *Religion in Life*, XXXI (1961), 356.

2. *Ibid*, p. 357.

3. Hamblett and Deverson, *Generation X* (New York: Fawcett Books, 1964), p. 33.

4. Allan R. Brockway, *The Secular Saint* (Garden City, N. Y.: Doubleday, 1968), p. 106.

4. Views on the State of the Church

1. C. I. Itty, "The Uniqueness of Christ in a World of Common Culture," Albert van den Heuvel, ed., *The New Creation and the New Generation* (New York: Friendship Press, 1965), pp. 82-83.

2. Abels, *op. cit.*, p. 7.

3. Roderick S. French, "Theological Reflections on the Church's Ministry to Youth," *The New Creation and the New Generation*, pp. 16-17.

4. Albert van den Heuvel, "A Short and Critical History of Youth Work," *The New Creation and the New Generation*, p. 54.

5. Itty, "The Uniqueness of Christ, . . ." p. 83.

6. Roy Larson and Charles E. Mowry, "Combined Report of Two Young Adult Consultations" (Nashville: General Board of Education of The Methodist Church, 1962), pp. 24-25.

5. Revolution in Piety

1. George D. Younger, *The Church and Urban Power Structure* (Philadelphia: Westminster Press, 1963), p. 78.

6. If the Medium Is the Message!

1. Marshall McLuhan and Quentin Fiore, *The Medium is the Massage* (New York: Bantam Books, 1967), p. 26.
2. Marshall McLuhan, *Understanding Media: The Extensions of Man* (New York: McGraw-Hill, 1965), pp. 8-9.
3. McLuhan and Fiore, *The Medium is the Massage*, p. 126.
4. *Ibid.*, p. 100.
5. *Ibid.*

7. The Key of Christian Mission

1. Ted McIlvenna, "Identification of Mission by Penetration" (Nashville: National Young Adult Project, 1967), p. 9.

8. The Church Can Help

1. Bob Fitch, *Hippie Is Necessary* (San Francisco: Glide Urban Center, 1967).
2. "Could You Answer My Question?" a 16mm black and white film which provides a profile of the active leadership of the new generation and an exploration of the search for appropriate mission methodology for contemporary urban society. Available from Audio-Visual Services, P. O. Box 871, Nashville, Tennessee 37202.

240

Mowry

AUTHOR

The Church and

TITLE

the New Generations

DATE LOANED	BORROWER'S NAME	DATE RETURNED